P9-DEG-692

MAXIMIZE THE MOMENT

ALSO BY T. D. JAKES

THE LADY, HER LOVER AND HER LORD

HIS LADY

T. D. JAKES

G. P. PUTNAM'S SONS

NEW YORK

MAXIMIZE

THE

MOMENT

God's

Action Plan

for

Your Life

Scripture quotations noted NKJV are from the New King James Version of
the Bible. Copyright 1979, 1980, 1982, Thomas Nelson, Inc., Publishers.
Scripture quotations noted NIV are from The Holy Bible, New International
Version. Copyright 1973, 1978, 1984 by International Bible Society. Used by
permission of Zondervan Publishing House. All rights reserved.

G. P. Putnam's Sons
Publishers Since 1838
a member of
Penguin Putnam Inc.
375 Hudson St.
New York, New York, 10014

Copyright © 1999 by T. D. Jakes
All rights reserved. This book, or parts thereof, may not
be reproduced in any form without permission.
Published simultaneously in Canada

ISBN 0-399-14565-6

BOOK DESIGN BY JENNIFER ANN DADDIO:

Printed in the United States of America

ACKNOWLEDGMENTS

There are a number of wonderful people who contributed in countless ways to my experiences in writing this book.

My gratitude to my family, who generously shared me with this manuscript. I will always appreciate your love and support. I also want to acknowledge the compassion and encouragement that I consistently received from my church family.

Thank you to Denise Silvestro, who tirelessly labored to enhance this project with her insights and creativity.

Thank you, Joel Fotinos, for your enthusiasm and for introducing me to the Putnam family.

Thanks also to A. Larry Ross and Associates, who helped to manage my schedule and protect my interests in innumerable ways.

Thank you to everyone at Putnam. You all treated me and my work with great dignity and integrity. My gratitude to Phyllis Grann, Susan Petersen Kennedy, Marilyn Ducksworth, Dan Harvey, Dick Heffernan, Martha Bushko, and everyone at JMS Marketing & Sales, Inc.

I would like to dedicate this book to my loving mother, Mrs. Odith P. Jakes, who died before its completion. Like the biblical character Rachel who died before her husband, Jacob, could complete his journey to Ephrata, my mother left before I could lay down my pen and conclude my thoughts on empowerment.

I wish to dedicate this book to the legacy she leaves behind—a legacy of pure excellence, tenacious living, sharpened intellect, and spiritual accuracy. She was the first public speaker who impressed me, the master teacher who singlehandedly impacted children and adults, motivating all who heard her to achieve their dreams.

She always said that I was a better teacher than she was. She bragged endlessly about my ability to illustrate an issue or articulate an abstract thought. I always smiled and wondered why she didn't realize I was simply following her teacher's manual every day of my life. She will be sadly missed, but never gone. As with all great teachers, she will live eternally in the hearts of those she taught. This is her book, and although I was often embarrassed when she said this publicly, I am forever her baby!

CONTENTS

MAXIMIZE THE MOMENT

INTRODUCTION

Somewhere between opulent monuments and historical artifacts, on a grassy green blanket of carefully manicured turf, lie the remains of America's thirty-fifth president. His untimely death left the nation saddened and shocked. His life was ended by a sniper's bullet that seemed to come from nowhere but which ultimately pierced the heart of every American. Across the country, newspapers were filled for weeks with heart-wrenching, gut-turning stories—a saga of tragedy, intrigue, and mayhem. But the real tragedy of that day will stay with all of us for time eternal.

Millions of Americans arose that morning thinking that this would be just another day, the same as others they had seen before. No one could have guessed that early foggy morning of November 22, 1963, that the day would end with secret service men running wildly to stop an event that was as cataclysmic as a meteor plummeting toward our planet. But by that night there was not a home in the nation that was not affected in some way by that terrible event. A nation lost its leader, the world lost a hero, and every man, woman, and child was reminded that fairytales do end—and sometimes it's not happily ever after.

A young life was cut short and a promising future shattered. President Kennedy's death drove home the words of Job: "Man born of a woman has but a few days" (Job 14:1, KJV). And it made us realize that those days can expire very quickly and without warning.

Not only had we lost our president, we had lost our naivete. John Kennedy was wealthy, privileged, and powerful, yet even he wasn't exempt from tragedy and trouble. And if he, with all his money, all his influence, and his secret service agents could be plucked from this life as easily as a ripe apple from a tree, then so could we. Watching the news coverage on television that night, we realized that we all are born of a woman and have but a few days.

President Kennedy was laid to rest (on November 25), and at his grave his wife Jacqueline bent down and lit a torch that would burn eternally to mark the end of a life that burned so very quickly. His life had blazed up and then burned out like a match. He exploded onto the pages of history and then extinguished as rapidly as he had ignited.

On his tomb a simple inscription is engraved:

John Fitzgerald Kennedy
1917–1963

The first date records when he entered into time. The second date marks his exit. The children he had raised, the education he had attained, the goals he had reached are encapsulated by one hyphen between those dates. All the loving he received and gave, all the challenges he overcame, all the men and women he motivated—all he accomplished is now simply a slash between two dates, a humble little blank. That is all life ends up being—the gap between dates etched on a stone, which most drive past and few stop to see.

Job was aware of this frailty. Solomon cried out in anguish, "Vanity of vanities, all is vanity" (Ecclesiastes 1: 2, NKJV). Solomon was a man who attained fame and recognition only to report that fulfillment in life is not found in grandeur and reputation alone. Both men leave strong warnings that we should maximize and prioritize our time and esteem it as precious, for life is fragile and fleeting. We need to make the most of the life God gave us today because tomorrow it may be gone.

These words might sound ridiculous to the young who think that life never ends. But the reality is simple: We are conceived in a blaze of passion and we enter this world in a flash of urgency, our life igniting quickly, erupting in flames of glory. We combust into various levels of splendor and then, in the blink of an eye, we burn out. Like JFK, we are mortal, and our life on this earth will eventually end.

Yes my friend, life is a hyphen locked between two dates. It is the gap between two appointments. We measure life in years like we measure water in cups and gallons. But what a miniscule measurement a cup is against an ocean. In the same sense, life is miniscule compared to eternity. Life is just a pause between notes in the symphony of the eternal.

I do not think that a person's life can be accurately measured by the number of days, for days lose their meaning when they stand in the face of eternity. No, the question isn't how *long* we live but how *well* we live. What matters are the moments we live life to the fullest. Like a child who wanders around a beach collecting seashells to carry back home, we gather events and moments that occur during our lives. We cannot hold on to days; they pass. But we can retain memories.

> Then he said to them, "Watch out! Be on your guard against all kinds of greed; a man's life does not consist in the abundance of his possessions." (Luke 12:15, NIV)

Nor can life be measured in the attainment of material possessions. Success should be applauded but not worshipped, acquired but not sought after. For you see, real success consists of more than riches alone.

In fact, riches are what you have, but wealth is what you are. You are wealthy in opportunities, wealthy in creativity, and wealthy in the chance to prioritize your life, maximize your potential, and reassess your strengths. You are wealthy because God loves you.

The other day I saw a bumper sticker that read, "Whoever dies with the most toys wins." It seems to me that when you're taking your last breath, you're not going to care how many toys you have. The kind of car you drive, the size of your office, the title on your business card—it all becomes meaningless at the end of your life. Many men and women climb the spiral staircase to success only to get to the last flight wishing they had spent more time with loved ones and friends. Neither stocks nor bonds, annuities or money markets will keep you warm in the winter of your life. There is no warmth in a ledger sheet or a company watch. You can't find comfort in a piece of gold or in all the diamonds in the world. Although we will and must achieve certain goals, and we will talk about how to do that effectively, we cannot forget the greater wealth of rich experiences that far exceeds the acquisition of temporal goods and services.

What is important is how we fill in the blanks between eternity past and eternity future. The dates are set by God and we cannot change them. I have seen a lot of people invest thousands of dollars in face lifts and tummy tucks, hair replacement and wrinkle removal. But the truth of the matter is we cannot un-age the aged. We cannot stop time. What we can do is control what we have control over, change what we can change, and survive what we cannot. In the end, a person is no more than the things he or she has done, the places he or she visited, and the events that occurred. Life is just a scrapbook of moments that have been collected. It does not matter how many days it took to collect the moments. All that matters in the end is what happened between eternity past and eternity future. All that matters is the hyphen between the dates.

FILL IN THE BLANKS

Remember when you were a student? There was one type of test we all dreaded. It wasn't the multiple-choice test. There was always a chance to guess some of those answers, or at least look for clues that would jar your memory and remind you of the information you studied. Then there were the essay questions, which provided a chance for you to drape your uncertainty in complex phrases and convoluted sentences. Use enough words and the teacher might not know you had no idea what the answer was. The most difficult questions to answer were not the true and false questions, since you had a fifty/fifty chance of being right no matter what you answered. None of these was the question that caused the weary heart of an ill-prepared student to skip a beat. It was always those fill-in-the-blank questions that would stump you every time. You either knew it or you did not. Oh, God help you if you didn't know the definite answer when the question demanded that you fill in the blank.

Perhaps that is what makes life seem so difficult. If you do not know the answer, my friend, you cannot fill in the blank. The answer is the thing we all seek to know while we live between the two dates. We need to know the answer or the blank is left empty and we die with a feeling of incompleteness. You and I have known people who reached the end of life with an incomplete over their heads. Wealthy but incomplete, attractive but incomplete, revered but incomplete—many fit in this category. But we cannot allow life to leave us with no credits for the days we spent.

We are born, and shortly thereafter we die, and all that lies between is a test that requires that each of us fill in the blank. Some fill it in with stellar accomplishments, others with the broadening of the intellect. Some fill it in with assisting the downtrodden, and some are determined to help only themselves. But regardless of which choice you make, the results will eventually lead you to the same thing. Sooner or later the bell rings, the test is over, and the sum total of what we did, and thereby who we are, is somewhere contained within the narrow space between entrance date and exit date. It is all in the blank between two points.

Judging the choices of others is not the highest and best use of our time. We will soon enough have to account for how we spent our own brief stay. It is not just a matter of facing some eternal judgment that seems too far off to be feared. Yes, I believe that judgment is imminent, but the truth is, in many ways we are being graded daily. We don't have to die to face the consequences of our decisions; we live with the results every day.

Who can say who scores the highest on the test of life? What's the best way to fill in the blank? I am not sure.

The other day I was driving down the interstate. It was a normal, busy day. I was trying to maximize my time, getting as much done as possible. I was driving with one hand and jotting down scribbled notes with the other. My mobile phone was on speaker so that I could finalize a few matters with my assistant. I was hurrying to a meeting and putting the final touches on documents with the information I was receiving over the phone.

I noticed that to my left there was a gentleman about my age driving in a car beside me. We were such a contrast. I was dressed in a navy blue business suit. My white shirt was crisp and my designer tie was meticulously in place. My head was aching a little, and I was tired from too many nights of too little sleep. He, on the other hand, looked completely refreshed. He was swaying to some music that was loud enough to hear through my closed windows. He was smiling and enjoying himself, almost oblivious to me and those around him. He was wearing a pair of shorts, an old T-shirt, and a baseball cap. He was driving a dented, older model automobile, which looked like it had seen better days. He seemed not to have a care in the world.

I pondered as I sped away from him, Who was really the most successful, he or I?

For unto whomsoever much is given, of him shall be much required: and to whom men have committed much, of him they will ask the more. (Luke 12:48, KJV)

The gentleman I saw in the other car obviously had less of everything than I did. He had less responsibility, less influence, and less demands. But he also had less stress, less fatigue, less anxiety, and less pressure. Who filled in the blank with the right answer? I concluded that we were both right. Life had asked us both a question, but we had chosen to fill in the blank totally differently.

Every decision is a matter of choosing what is right for you. Each choice has rewards and liabilities. You have to add them up and live with your decisions. I cannot make the decisions for you—no one can. The most important thing I can do is make you aware that the decision is yours to make. Yes, there are things that are beyond your control, but God has given us the gift to determine how we utilize the life He has bestowed on us.

The worst possible thing you can do is to fail to make a decision at all. Imagine yourself standing at the crossroads like a lost traveler deliberating endlessly over the options, unable to reach a decision about which way to go. Needless to say, you won't get anywhere.

There is only so much time you can spend in deliberation. Yes, you have to make sure the decision is your own and not someone else's opinion. Yes, you have to weigh the benefits and liabilities and determine if the decision is right for you. But eventually you need to act. One of life's greatest tragedies is to arrive at the end of your journey and realize you could have done more, laughed harder, played more intensely, and lived more vivaciously if only you had taken the day by the throat and steered it the way you wanted to go, if only you had made a conscious decision about what you wanted to do.

We all have to fill in the blank. We all have to take the same test. Life may just be a hyphen between two dates, but we want to make the most of it. The wisest thing we can do is minimize the liabilities, plan for the unexpected, enjoy the ecstasies, endure the disappointments, and then face the inevitable. In short, my counsel to you is simple: Always, absolutely always, maximize the moment!

Part One

———————————————— ⚙ ————————————————

MINIMIZE THE
MOMENT

ONE

———⟨⟩———

SAY WHEN

An elderly lady enters a local diner and approaches the nearest table. She drops her heavy parcels onto the floor and eases herself into the booth. She is tired and hungry. She has been running errands all morning and has stopped to get a cup of coffee and a donut before continuing on with her chores.

The diner is almost empty. A weary waitress shuffles over toward the woman's booth. She carries a steaming pot of coffee and automatically begins to fill her cup. The piping hot coffee begins to fill the expectant, up-turned cup, and the rich aroma wafts into the air. Almost as if she were talking to herself, the waitress mumbles, "Just say when." The coffee swirls wildly around the perimeter of the cup and quickly reaches the brim. It starts to overflow and splashes onto the table. The woman, who was only half-attentive, finally realizes that she had let it go too long before stopping the waitress. She smiles and says what should have been said a little sooner, "When."

The waitress had asked her to say when; she left the control of how much coffee was to be poured in the hands of the customer. But the woman was tired. She wasn't paying attention, and she expected the waitress to notice that the cup was filled.

More often than not, many of us sit quietly through life relying on others to see when the cup is filled. Like the cup, we are vulnerable to what people pour into us, but we tend to hope that they will see what they are doing to us and stop when it is too much. The truth of the matter is most people will keep dumping and dumping into you if you do not speak up.

People who don't speak up can find themselves in trouble because they didn't take control of the situation and speak up when they had had enough. They let people keep pouring on more problems, more burdens, more responsibilities. They didn't pay attention or else just kept their mouths shut, and before they know it, their life is overflowing with too much to do, too much heartache, and too much misery. They don't say anything and they wind up with nothing but one big mess to clean up.

Now it is true that you don't have to start a riot or drop a bomb on someone, but you do need to tell people when to stop. If something is not working for you, if someone is doing something you don't want them to do to you, you better take control of your life and be the one who says, "When."

Your life is too precious to leave it in the hands of someone else. You cannot expect someone else to take care of you. You cannot expect someone to tell you when you have had enough. We cannot trust our lives to anyone. God is the only one we can trust to steer our lives. Other people can act as advisors, but never allow someone's opinion to outweigh your own.

Empowerment begins when you take control of your life, when *you* recognize that you have had enough, when you take appropriate steps to make order out of what happens and when it happens in your life. You need to take your future out of the hands of bystanders and firmly grasp the reins. You'll have no control if you maintain your silence. You have to speak up and be heard. Lift your head, raise your voice, and shout out loud, "When!"

Overloaded people fail. They always have and they always will. They fail at marriage, ministry, and management. They fail at parenting, partnership, and professional endeavors. Like an airplane, we can only carry a certain amount of weight. If we have too much baggage on board, we will be ineffective and we won't be able to soar. Most people end up exceeding the weight limit. Motivated by the desire to please, impress, or otherwise gain commendation, they take on too much and, in the end, fail to reach the heights of success or else crash because they ignored their limitations.

In order to maximize your life, you have to minimize your load. You must decide what you will and will not take on. You must determine what is worthy of your attention. Every situation that arises does not deserve your attention. You must focus your concentration on what's important. Don't dilute it by spreading it too thin. Some things should be dismissed as just nuisances. I call them the gnats and flies of life. They are there to annoy you, like a flying insect you are tempted to swat at while driving. If you keep swatting at that fly, you may lose control of the car and end up in a wreck. You can only deal with so many things at one time. Choosing which to respond to and which to ignore helps you to maximize your life.

I have noticed that my grandmother has become less cranky with age. She doesn't get as upset as often as she once did. She doesn't lose her temper as easily. She has stopped rushing around trying to do everything and please everyone, and she's better off for it. I asked what brought about this change in her. She told me that she has come to realize that most things are not as important as they had once seemed. What she used to consider a crisis is now just an unfortunate incident. What she once thought absolutely necessary she now realizes is incon-

sequential. At this stage of her life, she has learned to distinguish what's important from the insects of life. Knowing which things to swat at is a sign of growing up and growing wise.

UNLOCK THE PRISON GATE

Lightening your load also means knowing when to release things. One of the most dangerous things is to be shackled to your past. We all make mistakes, we all have regrets, but we must learn how to move beyond them. Life is too short to allow yourself to be an inmate in the prison of bad choices and weak decisions. The prison of previous mistakes comes with jailers of guilt and regret. Together they hold you captive, torturing you with images of what you could have been and what you could have accomplished had you not done this or that or the other.

What's unfortunate is that most of us don't realize that the key to release ourselves is within our own hands. Often, we are our own wardens, prolonging the sentence. Actually, many times we are the judge, jury, and prosecutor, giving ourselves a life sentence of misery, mourning and regret. What we need to realize is that there is only one Judge, and He is forgiving.

> Let the wicked forsake his way,
> And the unrighteous man his thoughts;
> Let him return to the Lord,
> And He will have mercy on him;
> And to our God
> For He will abundantly pardon. (Isaiah 55: 7, NKJV)

Yes, we all make bad choices at one time or another, but all we need to remember is that if we ask the Lord for His forgiveness, He will be merciful and release us from our sins. So if our Father releases us from our sins, why do we remain in the self-imposed shackles of our past? Let us lift up our voices in repentance, and the walls of our prison cells will fall away.

I'm not saying you can just walk away from your mistakes. Sometimes there are consequences that we have to live with. However, when we make a bad choice, we need just apply the three Rs: We need to *repent,* try to *rectify* the situation, and take *responsibility* for our deeds. But once we do that, we need to move beyond the guilt.

SAY GOODNIGHT

You can't spend your life in the graveyard of guilt dealing with the corpses of the past. Know when things are dead, know when to release them and bury them. If you continue to work with the dry bones of dead issues, you, too, will begin to decay. No amount of work will resuscitate a corpse. Sign the death certificate and bury the past.

Some issues must be reckoned dead. It is neither weak nor cowardly to walk away from the past. Leaving behind dead issues does not mean you are quitting; it means you are conserving your strength for things that count, things you can change, things you can control. What do you gain by beating a dead horse? It is far braver and more beneficial to recognize that you must move ahead and face new challenges. Focus your energy on things you can actually make an impact on, and bury the past so it may rest in peace.

Some of you may remember *The George Burns Show.* George Burns ended each show with a simple, "Goodnight, Gracie." Sometimes that's all it takes—a simple goodnight. You just need to lay certain things to rest. I have spent countless hours counseling people who have lost precious moments of their lives because they were busy struggling with issues that should have been put to bed. How much more productive, how much more fulfilling, their lives could have been if they had just faced that lingering issue and said, "Goodnight, Gracie."

It is time to take inventory. Companies do it every day. Occasionally they write things off as a loss so that they can go on to make greater profits. Take stock of your life and determine which things are holding you back from profiting. Have the wisdom to recognize what is dead and have the courage to write it off.

TRIM THE EXCESS

In addition to shedding the past, to maximize your life you must also know how to cut yourself off from things that aren't working in the present. You need to constantly evaluate your life so that you can determine what is right in your life and what must be cast aside. God created you for a purpose, you are destined to accomplish certain things. Constantly ask yourself, "How does this relationship, this situation, this decision affect the overall outcome of my predestined purpose?"

I have seen people who didn't ask this question, or else didn't listen to the answer. They went through their lives surrounded by people and things that dragged them down and prevented them from reaching the heights of success. Their inability to trim the excess from their lives, to get rid of things that hindered instead of helped, caused them to wreck companies, destroy ministries, devastate children, and keep themselves from their life's goals. They were left bitter and old at the end of their lives when they could have been reveling in the success of a completed mission. They packed in too much mess and emptied out too few mistakes, and they were unable to complete their journey because their bags were too heavy and they wouldn't let them go.

PUT ON THE BRAKES

I believe that you must develop the habit of constantly taking inventory, and this will lead to an instinct of knowing when to say "when." You'll learn when to put on the brakes so that you don't crash and know when to keep going so that you stay on the road. You need to be in the driver's seat in your life. And part of being a competent driver is knowing when to apply the brakes. Who would want to drive a car that didn't have brakes?

I grew up in West Virginia. The mountains there are very high—they stand at attention like erect soldiers against the blue sky. When I was a boy, the roads along those mountains were winding and very rough. To navigate them you needed to be an adept and cautious driver. You can imagine how crucial it was to have good brakes as you spiraled wildly through and down those Appalachian Mountains. As a child, racing down those roads was more thrilling to me than any rollercoaster. As the car hugged the turns, the hair on the back of my neck would stand up and I would shut my eyes tightly and say a silent prayer that we made it through alright.

What if you didn't have brakes? Imagine the terror that would grip you as your car spun wildly out of control. In your mind, see your face distorted in a grimace of horror and your knuckles turning white as you clutch the steering wheel. Your heart races as you plummet down the mountainside. In a matter of seconds you move from fear to hysteria to the sad resignation that you are going to die.

Now think about the scenario I just described. There is one significant question: Why? You are not about to die because you didn't have a rich leather interior, power steering, air-conditioning, or a top-of-the-line sound system. No, you are dying because you were unable to brake. You lacked control. You can have a luxury model car with all the conveniences, but if there is no way for you to put on the brakes and stop the ride, you are at risk.

This is what happens when you don't exert control over your life. This is what happens when situations occur in your life and you just sit back and watch. You may think: I wish I had a better job; I wish I could leave this bad relationship; I wish I could complete this project. And so on and so forth. These are the collection of statements echoing in the heart of one who lacks control, one who cannot make liberating decisions, one who cannot grab the wheel, put on the brakes, and steer his life the way it is supposed to go.

Sometimes it is easier to let someone else do the driving. For a while, it may even be comfortable to sit back, relax, and enjoy the scenery. But you should not be a passenger in your life, at the mercy of someone else who is determining the route. God has given you the map; it is your calling to follow it. You cannot depend on someone else to chauffer you around. Others have a destination of their own. No matter how timid you are, you cannot allow anyone to dominate you and tell you where to go. Don't be trapped in the car or stuck in some wild car chase with no way to get out. Even well-meaning friends, your family, or your boss may try to determine your way. But get into the driver's seat and take hold of that wheel. Only you know where you have to go.

TAKING CONTROL

When talking about taking control, I must stress one thing: You should not, cannot, and do not need to control someone else's life; you just need to control your own. You cannot dictate what another person does, thinks, or feels. You can only be in charge of yourself. People may hurt you, whether it is an act of malice, indifference, or misdirection. Whatever the circumstances, you may not be able to stop another's actions, but you can minimize the effect it has on you. You can tell the person that you've had enough, that you will not stand for that treatment, and when necessary you can remove that person from your life.

Too often, our actions are dictated not by our own sense of purpose but by a misguided need to please. We want to make others happy and will do anything to win their approval. We care so much about what others think that with every step we take, we look over to see if our move is making someone smile. Although it is nice to be concerned for others, if you're always looking for approval, you're not looking where you're going and eventually you're bound to walk into a wall or trip over your own two feet.

We ought to obey God rather than men. (Acts 5: 29, NKJV)

The most important thing I can tell you is this: You do not have to please anyone except God, our Father. We are accountable to Him alone. Doesn't God tell us, "You shall have no other gods before Me"? Doesn't He tell us to have no idols, no false gods? You may say that you don't worship idols, but you do worship them when you dedicate your life to impressing others or when you allow the opinions of others to determine your actions. Those others become idols in your life.

Care not what others think and act only in accordance with the divine purpose you have received from God. Remember: To maintain control of your own life, you have to free yourself from the confines of public opinion. Keep to your plan and keep your life in your own hands.

Some of us don't exercise control over our own lives because we are too timid. We are afraid of speaking up and acting out. We question our right to say no. We ask ourselves, "Who am I to assert myself?" I ask you, Who are you not to? You are a child of God and as such you have the right to lead your life to its fullest.

What do you think will happen if you open your mouth and stand up for your rights? What are you afraid of? People I have counseled have told me that they worry that the people in their life will leave them if they say no. I say, let them go! People who have used and abused you won't be happy with your wanting to take control of your life. They've been in the driver's seat on this power trip and they won't want to give it up.

Well, people who don't respect your right to say "when," who don't honor your wish to stop, who don't understand when enough is enough are not worth the time of day. They're not worth a long, drawn-out discussion, they're not worth a major confrontation. Just get up, say goodbye, and walk out! You're better off without them. Don't waste another second. You might not be able to control their behavior, but as God as my witness, you can control your own.

STAY ON TRACK

Constantly take inventory of your life and determine what does and doesn't work for you. If you want to maximize your life and fulfill the plan that God has for you, you must take control of your life. Know when to say when, trim off the excess, and release yourself from the past. You cannot soar to great heights if you are weighted down with excess baggage. Learn to let go so you can fly.

TWO

‹—◦—›

PREDATORS AND
PARTNERS

We are not solitary creatures. Every day we interact with countless numbers of people—family, friends, neighbors, co-workers. God does not mean for us to be alone. He created Adam *and* Eve so that the two could be fruitful and multiply. He commanded Noah: "Of the birds after their kind, and of animals after their kind, and of every creeping thing of the earth after its kind, *two* of every kind will come to you to keep them alive" (Genesis 6:20, NKJV). Jesus said to his disciples: "For when two or three are gathered together in My name, I am there in the midst of them" (Matthew 18:20, NKJV).

Obviously, we are stronger in numbers. We are meant to live and work together. Joint efforts usually yield better results. To be most effective, we should come together, share our talents, motivate each other, and profit from the joyous unity of like-minded individuals who share their skills, their hearts, and their lives.

However, not all relationships serve to benefit us. There are some relationships that should be avoided. They sap your life away and weaken your focus. If you are going to maximize your life, you need to recognize these toxic relationships and know when to walk away from them. We need to be vigilant about the company we keep and learn to sever those ties that strangle us—associations that are filled with turmoil, affiliations that need continuous maintenance, alliances that undermine.

A toxic relationship can be like a bad leg that is gangrenous. If you don't amputate it, the infection will spread throughout your entire body. The bitter bile of one bad relationship can seep into every other aspect of your life. It can destroy your family, bankrupt your business, and blacken your heart. People who do not have the courage to cut off what will not heal will eventually end up losing so much more.

CUT OFF CONFLICT

There are several types of relationships that you need to identify as liabilities. One of the most obvious to spot is one in which there is constant disagreement and strife. You interact like two armies on the battlefield, opposing sides in a war of words and a battle of wills. One says black, the other says white. One says up, the other says down. It seems like the only thing you can agree upon is that you disagree.

A relationship of this sort consumes all of your energy. You spend so much time arguing that you barely have strength for anything else. How much more productive you could be if you didn't have to spend all your time debating and defending your position. Relationships that are full of conflict suck the life out of you. They kill your dreams and pollute your future. They rob you of your will to achieve. They are enemies of greatness, sabotaging your attempts to achieve your full potential by getting you mired in meaningless minutiae and keeping you preoccupied by the frivolity of aimless arguments.

When you and someone in your life are embroiled in continuous disagreement, it is sometimes better to dissolve that association. It makes no sense to be involved with someone who brings you no joy and hinders your success. Why navigate your boat through the choppy waves of endlessly turbulent relationships? Instead, leave behind the stormy seas and seek calmer waters. You won't get anywhere if you are surrounded by people who inhibit your forward movement.

WHEN IT'S WORTH THE STRUGGLE

Now, I want you to understand that there are some difficult relationships that are worth struggling to maintain. There are connections with children and parents in which unconditional love makes us endure the pain. We are bonded with our parents who through the good grace of God conceived us and brought us into this world. We are commanded to obey them, and in accordance with God's law we should seek to avoid conflict with them whenever possible.

> *Honor your father and your mother, that your days may be long upon the land which the Lord your God is giving you. (Exodus 20:12, NKJV)*

Similarly, the Bible teaches that children are to be valued and loved without condition. Nowhere is this illustrated more clearly than in the story of the prodigal son (Luke 15:11–32). Here Jesus tells of a man whose son goes out into the world and squanders his fortune. Yet, upon the son's return home, penniless and ashamed, the father welcomes him with open arms. No matter what he has done, he is still the man's son and as such is welcomed home. Likewise, we should always greet our children with open arms. They may stumble and veer off the path, but as their parents, we should follow our Father's example and love our children unconditionally.

Now, one may ask, what about marriage? Am I telling you that you should get a divorce if you and your spouse are having a challenging time? No, that is not what I mean. Every marriage has its struggles, but marriage is sealed with an oath that promises to withstand good times and bad. Marriage is a sacred vow and a contract between hearts that have committed to weather the seasons of life together. Whether they face the cold blight of winter or the parched heat of summer, they are committed to stand together.

I have written more extensively about this in other books, and I urge you to read those words with an open mind and an accepting heart if you are experiencing traumatic marriage troubles. I also encourage to you to get pastoral counseling. However, the next time disagreement raises its ugly head in your marriage, I offer this advice: Talk, talk, and talk some more. Communicate so that you understand each other's needs and perspective. Simple words may be all you need to ease conflict out of your life.

THAT WAS THEN, THIS IS NOW

A relationship does not have to be tumultuous to be a liability. Sometimes what seems to be a pleasant and familiar association can be one that holds you back from achieving your full potential. Specifically, I am talking about alliances that are rooted in shared pasts and bound together by common memories. You can laugh together about old times, you can reminisce about days gone by. Like a pair of old shoes, these relationships are comfortable. Yet if these shoes are worn, with holes in the soles, how far are they going to get you on your journey? And if these relationships are based on nothing but old ties, how can they take you into a successful future? They may anchor you to a former life and prevent you from moving ahead.

A common past is good. It unites your yesterdays. But common goals are better: They unite your tomorrows. Many people come from the same background, even grow up in the same home, and wind up in a completely different place in life. Just because you started out together doesn't mean you're supposed to be together today. How much better it is to share common goals for the future, so you can pull each other along instead of holding each other back.

It is sad to realize, but often people who knew you way back when do not have the ability to know you now. They generally assess your potential based on their perspective of your past.

> *Coming to his hometown, he began teaching the people in their synagogue, and they were amazed. "Where did this man get this wisdom and these miraculous powers?" they asked.*
>
> *"Isn't this the carpenter's son? Isn't his mother's name Mary, and aren't his brothers James, Joseph, Simon and Judas?*
>
> *"Aren't all his sisters with us? Where did this man get all these things?"*
>
> *And they took offense at him. But Jesus said to them, "Only in his hometown and in his own house is a prophet without honor."*
>
> *And he did not do many miracles there because of their lack of faith.*
> *(Matthew 13: 54–58, NIV)*

Jesus did not do many miracles in his hometown. It was not the geographic location that hindered his performance. Rather, he held back because of the limited vision of those who were more acquainted with his past than his present. They recognized his "wisdom" and observed his "miracles," but their opinion reverted to what they had known of him before. Jesus responded to that by leaving. He could have done more had they had faith, but faith is futuristic, and they were stuck in a historical perspective of who and what he had been to them.

Some of you are being held back by an "I-knew-you-when" crew. They keep you stuck in a stage of your life that is past and gone. These people define you on the basis of who you were, not who you have become, and certainly not who you can someday be. These old-time relations rob you of the momentum you need to soar; they do not permit you to embrace the future because they want to keep you in the past.

God wants to do great things in you, but you need to move beyond the "good old days." This might be difficult. You might miss the strolls down memory lane. But folks from the past may want you to linger too long on that path. They may want you to set up house and stay a while. You can't do this if you want to maximize your life.

It is a gift to have people in your life who know where you've come from *and* can relate to where you're going. You will be lucky to have some relationships like this. But if you have to sacrifice one or the other, remember, the past is over and cannot be rewritten; it can only be played out over and over again. Stop rehearsing the beginning and write the rest of your story. The future is before you like an uninhabited land waiting for the pioneers of destiny to explore it. Forge ahead!

PREDATORS OF THE HEART

Perhaps the most dangerous relationship is the one most difficult to spot. I'm talking about the stealthy, stalking, night-walking burglars who prey on your heart and rob you of control. These aren't black-cloaked ghouls with hideous, blood-curdling screams, which torture and terrorize you. No, they are much more terrifying than that. They are seemingly kind, apparently loving, whispering flattering words and sweet promises, which make your cheeks blush and your heart go pitter-patter. They are the proverbial wolves in sheep's clothing.

We've all known people like this. They say what we want to hear and bat their eyelashes with an innocence that belies their true intentions. They take advantage of our need to be loved and accepted, and manipulate us into doing what they want. These are the co-workers who outwardly praise us, then sabotage our work to advance their own careers. They are the lovers who promise to leave their wives but never intend to keep that promise. They are the so-called friends who encourage us to just try the drug once—it couldn't hurt—and then so obligingly sell it to us when we become addicted.

They are false friends and malicious manipulators, who lead you to believe they are acting in your best interest, when in fact they're not thinking of you at all. Recall the serpent in the Garden of Eden. He engaged Eve in conversation and beguiled her with lies cloaked in smooth words.

> *Now the serpent was more subtle than any beast of the field which the LORD God had made. And he said unto the woman, Yea, hath God said, Ye shall not eat of every tree of the garden? And the woman said unto the serpent, We may eat of the fruit of the trees of the garden: But of the fruit of the tree which is in the midst of the garden, God hath said, Ye shall not eat of it, neither shall ye touch it, lest ye die. And the serpent said unto the woman, Ye shall not surely die: For God doth know that in the day ye eat thereof, then your eyes shall be opened and ye shall be as gods, knowing good and evil. (Genesis 3: 1–5, KJV)*

The serpent knew exactly how to entice the first man and woman. The sneaky snake knew that he could twist and distort the truth of God—who simply wanted His Creation to obey because He knew what was best for them. Like a clever actor delivering an award-winning performance, the Enemy preyed on the weaknesses of Eve and Adam: their desire to be loved and valued, their desire to feel good in the moment without considering who their Lord had created them to be. Can't you just hear that hissing tongue whispering, "Why, God doesn't want you to eat that fruit because if you do, you'll be just like him! Go ahead, it's the sweetest, juiciest fruit you'll ever taste!"? Instead of clinging to God's warning and trusting Him, the first couple were blindsided and bit into Satan's lies.

It's the same bite of the apple we're taking when we listen to the smooth-talkers in our lives who convince us to ignore God's love and forget who we are. They beguile us with charm by telling us what we want to hear in the moment. It's the temptation to think we're either more than human—as if the Creation ranked equal with the Creator— or that we're less than human, that we need whatever poison the snake-charmers have to offer: the allure of wealth, the promise of power, the gratification of illicit love. No, we are men and women created in God's image with precious, eternal value.

> *What is man that You are mindful of him, and the son of man that You visit him?*
> *For You have made him a little lower than the angels, and You have crowned him*
> *with glory and honor. (Psalm 8:4–5, NKJV)*

We must remain ever vigilant for those predators who smile and whisper soothing words, hypnotizing us with deceptive charm while all along exploiting, exhausting, and extinguishing our God-given, pur-poseful identity. Never forget that you are God's child, a son or daugh-ter of the King of Kings, who is created a little lower than the angels. He has given you a unique and privileged purpose that belongs to no one else. Do not be fooled into compromising your royal identity to street-smart con artists with bright but poisonous apples up their sleeves.

"C" YOUR WAY CLEAR

As we all know, severing relationships that are harmful sounds easier than the reality of doing it. It's also much easier to cut loose the rela-tionships with people who overtly drag us down, who remain stuck in the past, or who have proven untrustworthy. However, for most relationships, it's usually much more difficult to discern the complexity of the interaction. I recall reading my daughter the story of Little Red Riding Hood. Can you remember the part of this children's classic where the Big Bad Wolf convinces Red Riding Hood to take her time going to Grandma's house? "Go ahead," says the Wolf, "pick your Grandma some flowers, take the scenic route through the forest. You've got plenty of time." Well, when you come to that part of the story, most bright children will ask, "Daddy, why didn't Little Red Riding Hood know that the Wolf was up to no good? Didn't she know that Wolves are bad?" But it is one thing to know there are wolves out in the world who want to harm us, and it's another thing to recognize them when they cross our paths.

The innocent question of an inquisitive child is one a mature adult could well afford to consider and benefit from. I continually take inventory of the people around me. Are there wolves encouraging me to dawdle along my life's path, wolves dressed up like sweet Grandmas trying to deceive me so they can eat me up? Unfortunately, most of us have these kinds of people preying on us. And if real-life relationships were as clear-cut as fairy tales, then we could easily run away or denounce those wolves. But the challenge comes in evaluating the people around us, because we all know that some conflict is inevitable, even with the people we love who truly love us. So we must constantly ask ourselves about the ultimate motives and bigger pictures when we experience trials in our relationships. I believe there are four Cs that help us to see our way clear and take action: *Confront, Correct, Compromise,* or *Cut Off.*

FACING THE PHARISEES

Most of us do not like confrontations. They usually involve anger and heartache, sore tempers, and swollen egos. You may even think all confrontations end up as bitter arguments with hurt feelings that linger like deep bruises on the heart. But a true confrontation of those people in our lives who trouble us is a necessary, God-ordained part of relating as human beings. "Confront" simply means to see clearly and face directly the essence of a particular relationship. We must be willing to see others for who they are and what they are committed to. If they are not committed to our ultimate good, then we may need to confront and expose them. Our Savior knew this and was not afraid to confront anyone, especially those who felt threatened by His love and mercy: the Pharisees.

> Then Jesus spoke to the multitudes and to His disciples, saying: "The scribes and Pharisees sit in Moses' seat. Therefore whatever they tell you to observe, that observe and do, but do not do according to their works, for they say, and do not do. For they bind heavy burdens, hard to bear, and lay them on men's shoulders; but they themselves will not move them with one of their fingers. But all their works they do to be seen by men . . ." (Matthew 23:1–5a, NKJV)

Our Lord then goes on to list the many evidences of the Pharisees' self-righteous, self-serving, prideful behavior. We have to keep in mind that these were some of the most powerful, influential religious leaders of His day. But Jesus recognized that some of them were only concerned about looking good, about following the letter of the law, and not about loving His heavenly Father and serving others with His love. Certainly, confronting these powerful vipers was not easy. However, by His willingness to consistently see these men for who they really were, not who they pretended to be, Jesus reminds us that confrontations require *character, courage,* and *caution.*

Since Jesus is secure in His identity as God's own Son, He is free to let go of the need to please and be accepted by those around Him. He doesn't need the pat on the back from these deceptive deacons at the door of the church to feel good about himself and His standing with the Lord.

Grounded in who we really are, in who our gracious Father created us to be, allows us the freedom to confront as necessary without worrying about negative consequences.

Second, what phenomenal courage we see exercised by our Lord Jesus as He confronts this group of the religious elite. Although they have the power to undermine His reputation, which leads to His death on the cross, Christ faces them squarely and calls them at their game. Certainly, the consequences of His actions were much more severe than most of ours. Nevertheless, we must take up our cross daily and follow the Savior, even when it means confronting those who are secretly our enemies.

Finally, we must use caution when we confront others. Now, you may be saying, "Wait a minute. Didn't you just tell me to be courageous and tell others how we see them?" Yes, I did, but we must balance that courage against caution in order to make sure we are following God's timing and not our own. It's easy to use false courage, or bravado, to challenge others just to get our way. It's so easy to claim a confrontation with another is necessary when really we just want to take control of the situation. No, we must prayerfully ask God to show us when, how, who, and where to confront others. We must balance our fears of confrontation with courage, and our own selfishness with wise caution. The best way to do this is to come back to where we started with Jesus' example: character. Remembering who we are as children of the King enables us to see others for who they really are and to address them face-to-face when necessary.

SALVAGING THE SILVER

A young woman once bought an intricately designed pair of candlesticks at a yard sale for one dollar. They were a dark, dingy gray color, and the young lady assumed that they were made of pewter or some other blackish metal that warranted the inexpensive price. She took them home, gave them a dusting, and set them on her dining room table with an elegant white candle in each one. Some months later, a friend who worked in an antiques store was over for coffee with the young lady. "When are you going to get around to cleaning those candleholders, girl?" asked her friend. "Why, I dusted them just yesterday," replied the startled hostess. "Dusted?" laughed her friend. "These things need to be polished! They're silver—only that awful tarnish keeps them from shining the way God intended!" The two friends got silver polish and clean cloths and rubbed over and over until the dull charcoal metal yielded a gleaming pair of beautiful silver candlesticks. The young lady had appreciated the candleholders before, but now she couldn't take her eyes off the craftsman's artistry!

Sometimes our relationships are like that pair of dingy, tarnished candlesticks. We assume that a relationship is what it appears to be and therefore don't expect much from it. We let surface appearances, quick-to-judge labels, fears of confrontation, and laziness produce complacency. If only we were willing to go beyond the surface impression and truly evaluate the substance from which the relationship is forged, we may discover a true treasure. And if we don't, and the relationship is as it appears, then we can more accurately assess whether or not it is worth keeping.

Like the word "confrontation," correction often has negative associations in our minds and hearts. We assume the word means that we are wrong, or that someone else is wrong (which may bring us back to confrontation again!), and that something has to be done about it. While this may be true, we often fail to see the true potential waiting underneath the coat of tarnish.

Too often we're so afraid that a good friend will reject us if we point out a correctable fault. Although she may react defensively, our friend may eventually be thrilled to realize that you care more about her ultimate well-being than about her immediate response to you. Corrections made from a loving spirit, not a self-righteous, I-know-what's-best attitude, are often well received. If others sense that you are genuinely concerned for them and long for a better, deeper, more holy relationship with them, they are likely to consider what you have to say and make appropriate changes.

Similarly, we must be willing to receive correction from those who love us as well. Consider King David at the height of his power as well as his sinfulness. First he seduces another man's wife, and then he has her husband murdered. David is sorely unhappy but cannot see past his pride as king to turn back to the Lord. It takes the love of his friend and advisor Nathan to help him see his sinful mistake and return to God's path. After Nathan wisely tells David a story of a poor man being robbed of his only lamb by a rich man with many flocks, King David is outraged at the injustice and then realizes the parallel to his own theft. "Then David said to Nathan, 'I have sinned against the Lord.' And Nathan said to David, 'The Lord also has put away your sin; you shall not die'" (2 Samuel 12:13, NKJV).

God often uses us in each other's lives to restore us to the narrow, yet rich, paths of destiny that He has preordained. Honest and gentle rebuke motivated by love increases trust, communication, and integrity in both the giver and receiver. "My Son, do not despise the chastening of the Lord, nor be discouraged when you are rebuked by Him; for whom the Lord loves He chastens, and scourges every son whom He receives" (Hebrews 12:5–6, NKJV). Ask yourself which of your relationships need some correction. There may be some people who need to correct you as well. In both cases, we must be committed to God's ultimate purposes in our beings in order to rub away the gray grime of accumulated tarnish and salvage the sparkling silver sheen underneath.

HEALTHY COMPROMISE

Sometimes relational discernment is not just a matter of confronting those who are against you or correcting those who lack wisdom or have slipped from the grasp of God's Truth; sometimes confrontation and correction must lead to healthy compromise. Before I explain further, let me first define compromise in this instance. I do not mean compromise in the sense of giving up what you truly believe, or who you truly are. I do not mean taking shortcuts and resigning yourself to second- or third-best because you're impatient or afraid.

No, healthy compromise is about learning to negotiate win-win possibilities within relationships. This often means seeing things through the eyes of the others involved in a situation or problem. When I was younger and enjoyed playing my favorite music as loud as my speakers would allow, I did not take time to think about my neighbors in the apartments around me. If they complained, I apologized but secretly assumed that it was a generational thing and they were just too old to appreciate my music. Now that I'm older and a bit wiser, I know what it means to be the neighbor on the other side of the wall. It's no fun when the baby you've been rocking to sleep is awakened by a deafening guitar riff or when you have to work the morning shift and a steady bass beat is pounding through your head at 3 A.M.

Both neighbors have needs and rights, but they both have to learn to get along in order to function as a community. Sometimes it's okay to crank up the music and dance on the living room floor. But it's also good to think of others and turn it down or even off after a reasonable hour.

In most cases of healthy compromise, both parties may feel that they are "right." Both you and another person may intend the best for each other. You both may believe firmly that you are fulfilling the Father's in-structions for your lives, and for the issue under discussion. This is when it's tempting to dismiss each other as "wrong" or "selfish" and refuse to see any other viewpoint but your own. However, this is when it is most crucial to relinquish pride, to step outside of the roles you're playing, and to become the other person. Can you see the legitimacy of his point of view? Can you appreciate why she might feel that way? Can you help him or her to understand your position in the same manner?

"Lord, You will establish peace for us, for You have also done all our works in us." (Isaiah 26:12, NKJV)

Be at peace among yourselves . . . See that no one renders evil for evil to anyone, but always pursue what is good both for yourselves and for all. (1 Thessalonians 5:13b, 15, NKJV)

The Lord's peace often results from each side coming closer to His viewpoint, His perfect plan for both parties. Healthy compromise is the hallmark of healthy relationships. If we are so entrenched in our point of view that we cannot change or adapt, then we become like a meadow's pond cut off from springs of clear-flowing water, stagnant and lifeless, covered with the green surface scum of our own pride. Sim-ilarly, we must know when not to compromise too far. We must not allow someone else's insistence to wear away or replace our true heart convictions. We must not allow someone else to dam up our water sup-ply, which once again would lead to still-water stagnation. We need to focus on God's perspective, to stay attuned to those things that truly matter most, and encourage others to do the same. With this kind of viewpoint, we keep the water moving, fed by springs of loving commu-nication and resolution. Suddenly, the little things don't seem so im-portant; we realize what we can and cannot live without. We learn that it's more important to love our neighbor well than to be deafened by our favorite tune. Sometimes a little give-and-take will make the relationship work for everyone involved.

ALWAYS OFF-KEY

In music, harmony is achieved from diverse notes that, though different in pitch, are nonetheless related and committed to producing a pleasant sound to the ear. Like music, some relationships only need fine-tuning and rehearsing, and through the processes of confrontation, correction, and compromise, they may finally produce the sweetest song. However, some relationships produce dissonance no matter how many times the instruments are tuned or how often the notes on the page are rehearsed. No matter how hard you or they try, the resultant notes are always off-key.

What causes such discord? If there is no common purpose, you have no rhythm to keep you in step with the band. Ultimately, someone is going to have to walk away. There should be a common goal. We work best when we feel the same pull of destiny. It is that magnetic force that pulls us together and unites us in common goals. It's not having attended the same university or sharing the same taste in clothes, not the same socio-economic background or favorite sports team. You must share the same goals and ambitions if the music is to find its harmony. If not, the results sooner or later will be disastrously shrill and grating.

Or consider these off-key relationships this way. Imagine a set of Siamese twins tied together trying to go in two different directions. That is what your life will be like if you are tied to people who want one thing while you want another. You will not be able to walk "together." Your Siamese relationships, those that have you tied to people, require that they are people who are in cooperation and not competition with you.

It is difficult as you succeed in life to find people who are not in competition with you but who remain in cooperation with your goals and objectives. Cooperation, in essence, means that the two of you co-*operate* well together. Competition, on the other hand, diminishes and destroys the team spirit of cooperation. When you find yourself tied to someone who is secretly jealous of or competitive with you, they sap your energy: It's like trying to swim in the ocean with a hundred-pound weight tied to your feet. As hard as it may be, you must cut the dead weight and swim freely to the golden shore ahead.

WHEN IT'S TIME TO SAY GOODBYE

Although it's not an easy decision to make, there are usually some signals you will notice that forecast the need to choose the direction of your associations. While it is impossible to survive without partnerships, it is also impossible to partner with people who do not share the same intensity and the same objectives. Notice that both are needed: Intensity focuses on how badly we want it while objectives focus on the specificity of what we want. These two key ingredients are as essential to winning partnerships as chocolate chips and cookie dough are to one of my favorite treats. Without the intensity of that burst of chocolate when you bite into the warm, home-baked cookie, the taste is disappointingly bland. And without the cookie part to anchor the chocolate chips, the experience is too sweet and rich. No, it takes both parts to produce the desired, balanced results. Most problems with the recipe for winning relationships stem from divisions in these two crucial areas.

First, the lack of intensity is frustrating when a very focused, intense person is tied to someone who is less driven and more complacent. It's like trying to dance the Macarena with someone who only wants to waltz. You have one tempo for life while your partner has another. When tempos are not compatible, your energies are divided because you spend all of your much-needed effort trying to motivate the partner to follow your lead and pick up the pace. You will lose accomplishment eventually because you are wasting time, expecting them to be something that they are not.

I have learned that listening is a key tool in any relationship. If you listen, people generally tell you who they are before you get involved. In the past, I have been so quick to encourage that I didn't listen to people who, as I reflect back on it, had warned me of their weaknesses beforehand. But I was so busy encouraging them and being polite that I disagreed with their assessments and confessions, and I failed to realize that they knew themselves better than I did. Instead, I should have listened and kept my positive-thinking, motivational "Oh-no-that-can't-be-true" thoughts to myself. In the end, it was true, and I realized that they had told me in so many words what to expect, and I had missed the signals. Please learn the priceless art of listening to people without interrupting them. It will save you years of tears and secret disappointments.

If you just listen, you will save yourself the pain of many negative experiences. But I must warn you that more times than not we use our optimism or persuasive style to coerce others into accepting our goals and objectives. But they cannot run off of your fuel, nor can they become something just because you believe that they can. They must possess their own faith for the many challenges that are always along the way to accomplishment. It is often a bad sign if you have to jump-start them every day. Like a car with a dry cell in its battery, if they do not hold a charge it may be a sign of a deeper trouble. You must decide if it's worth the effort to take on a life-long process of resuscitating them every week or two.

Without your awareness of this problem, these high-maintenance relationships can often weary you and exhaust your strength for years.

However, you must remember that anyone you have to keep motivating to get started, you may have to motivate to maintain. This is generally true in private as well as professional relationships. These are high-maintenance relationships. It is difficult to get anyone to run off of someone else's adrenaline. Tragically they will soon run out of your gas. In a slow, downward motion, they will decelerate, because it is impossible to fuel someone else's journey from your own incentives. Inevitably, they must have their own motivation and inspiration, and they must be self-contained, self-fueling locomotives that move from inner combustion.

PASSION FOR YOUR PURPOSE

It is lethal when you are surrounded by people who have an attitude of indifference about the goal that you have laid down to attain in your life. There are some issues that can be corrected through teaching and leadership, but you cannot teach someone to care. The person who doesn't have the passion for your purpose is in the wrong place. They will destroy the workplace, ruin your productivity, and hinder the rhythm of your company with complaining and murmuring. In a marriage, they are strychnine. In a friendship, they are constantly dissatisfied.

How can you tell if someone shares your dreams, goals, and hopes for the future? I look for the twinkle in your eye when you discuss the focus of our relationship. That twinkle in your eye is the unmistakable passion that ignites the soul and keeps you ablaze. The motivation has to be more than the money in a business transaction. It has to be more than the sex or status or financial gain in a marriage.

Look for that inner spark of passion simmering within—not just a burst of initial enthusiasm that can be feigned. Never walk with anyone anywhere who has no passion for the thing you are going to do together.

Your basic purpose has to be the same or your progress will be impeded. "Can two walk together, except they be agreed?" (Amos 3:3, KJV). This rhetorical question in the Book of Amos suggests that the obvious answer is no. It makes me think of a brigade of men marching in their uniforms and stepping proudly in a synchronized method. There are many feet, but they sound like one because they are not only outwardly uniformed but also inwardly synchronized. Imagine now, as they step in such a precise manner, if one of them is out of step. It ruins the presentation of the whole brigade. They break the rhythm and the cycle of movement by stepping out of the adopted rhythm of the other men. You have seen it on the job, in a marriage, in many areas of life. We must say goodbye to these kinds of people and seek out others who hear the same tune we hear and, while they may play different instruments, share our tempo.

3-D PARTNERSHIPS

If you understand that dissension and endless disagreements are powerful tools that distract creative people from building and progressing, then by the same token, please consider that unity—what I call 3-D partnerships—is just as powerful in assisting you in attaining goals. If you can walk with people whose life goals are similar, you will be amazed at their contribution. Now, let us be succinct in this subject. You are not trying to find people who are gifted in the same way as you, nor are you searching for people who are gifted to the same degree. Many times you can receive from someone whose gift is in its infancy but is there nonetheless. I am not sure that we should seek out people, anyway. Just recognize who life sends us and develop the ability to quickly access what type of relationship it is. Some you let pass by you like boats passing a port. They could dock, but if they are going somewhere else, let them go. You don't want to become a people seeker. Some people spend their whole life looking for the "right" people. I want to give you some concepts that will help you make better choices when someone does come your way.

CELEBRATING DIVERSITY

The first of the three D's requires that we remain open-minded and not succumb to our fears of others' differences. The people you relate with do not have to be a carbon copy of you to be a pollen-carrier. People often look for others who are synonymous with them rather than harmonious with them. That is not productive. These relationships are not fruitful, only familiar. Often we choose people who do what we do because the conversation is easy and we understand what each other is like. The problem is there will be no fruit because there is no "cross" in the pollination process.

Accepting and appreciating the differences of others provides us with new data about the world. It stimulates and challenges us to get out of our ruts and appreciate the many wonderful spices God has provided through each different man, woman, and child. I once knew a gentleman who started attending our church in West Virginia. He was the first of a long line of Caucasian people who started attending and ultimately ended up joining our church. Although we had had several Caucasians who joined us because they appreciated our ministry or the message, his reasons went a little further. He said, "I am just tired of being around people who dress like me, look like me, think like me. My life is boring. I want to see the many facets of God and life. I appreciate what I have, and those of my own status, race, and place. But I am tired of living in a microcosm, a carefully controlled environment that doesn't allow me the opportunity for real meaningful exchange." He was saying that his life was bland, like sitting down to eat a plate full of food that had no variety. You want the meal to be harmonious, but who wants to eat the same dish every day?

It's natural to be attracted to others like yourself. Builders like to interact with other builders. Singers like to interact with other singers. Preachers enjoy other preachers. Lawyers meet together for dinner or to play golf. But if you look closely, many times these relationships are difficult to maintain. Relationships are most productive when we interact with people who complement us without duplicity. When they do work, it is, for instance, generally two preachers whose strength is in different arenas. Or two doctors who are not competitive for the same clients or services. If the similarities have no distinction, the relationship requires a lot of maintenance. It is not impossible but more complicated to maintain. They also need a mutual respect for each other intellectually or there is no room for exchange. Why should I drink from the pool of your wisdom if I secretly think you are a fool?

Any investment broker worth his salt will advise you to diversify your investments. You do not put all of your funds in one stock. Relationships are investments. They require time and energy and they yield returns. If preachers would interact with counselors, they could share diverse perspectives on issues related but not duplicated. They will see a larger return on their investment. They will have a greater sense of harvest because they are similar enough to be related but diverse enough to be stimulating.

It is unwise to surround yourself only by people who think just like you. You do need to be in harmony, but there is a difference between harmony, which is derived from two distinctly different notes that blend together, and unison, the same note made at the same time. Harmony is far more appealing to the ear than unison. Your relationships should be harmonious without being in unison.

ARE YOU GOING MY WAY?

The second of the three D's is direction. We need others who are differ-ent from us but who share the same long-term goals and mission. Di-verse people moving in different directions would not be very productive. Instead, it is the diversified, complementary team working together in appreciation of each one's contribution to the end goal that makes the partnership work. No company could afford to hire all typ-ists. A restaurant cannot be operated if everybody hired is a chef. You need diversity of function but agreement of direction.

Many people have not yet opened their mind to appreciate that oth-ers who are different from them are just as valuable in arriving at the same destination. Without diversity in the same direction, these people are robbing themselves culturally, emotionally, and spiritually. I recall a friend who was seeking companionship. He said, "I will only date some-one who has as much money as I do." I looked at him and laughed. I said, "I have noticed your life for some time and I can see your great wealth. But I am telling you that in many ways you are the poorest person I have ever met." He looked shocked. I explained, "You have no one to make you laugh, no one to challenge you intellectually or emotionally. You have a bunch of paid by the hour yes-men who are basically ro-bots." His eyes filled with tears. He knew I was right. He was about to go out and get more of what he already was. I told him, "You can find some-one who is talented, gifted, and successful in some way without it being the same way as yours. You can find someone who has what you lack. You see, all fruitful relationships are the result of exchanging strengths, not duplicating them."

My friend had become accustomed to the false notion that those different from himself could not possibly be going in the same direction. He hadn't yet realized that the question is not, "Are you just like me?" but rather, "Are you going my way?" That is the question that matters more.

You want someone who is going your way. If you are going to be ultimately effective and maximize your moment, you need people who have the same directional agreement. They may not do everything the way you do, but they must have the same directional thrust. They should be people who are on their way. People who have direction and goals understand commitment and tenacity. People who do not share your directional thrust are weights and albatrosses around your neck, and they will cause you to sink.

DELIBERATE DESTINATION

The third of the three D's involves the commitment to working together in fulfilling the common goal: a deliberate destination. You may appreciate diverse people and include many in your partnerships who are headed in your same direction. Without a deliberate commitment to each other from all sides, however, the end goal cannot be fulfilled. Consider driving on the interstate. I can be driving in the same direction as a lot of other diverse people, yet we each have separate agendas and specific destinations. Eventually, you take your exit in your direction and I take mine. However, if we are part of a convoy that has clearly communicated our need for one another and our commitment to make sure everyone arrives at our destination, then we will work together. I will make sure you follow my lead, or I will make sure that your taillights remain in view as I follow you. It's the only way we're all going to reach our final destination: if we make sure that we help each other along the way, sharing strengths and compensating for weaknesses, in fulfilling our common goal.

Jesus recognized the importance of these three D's to fulfilling His Father's business on this planet. The first thing our Lord did when he got ready to redeem the world was to organize a team. He was the key agent for the redemption, but he still had a group of people who had the same directional focus. The team was diverse: a tax collector, a physician, and a fisherman. Finally, they were committed to a deliberate destination.

Jesus knew that He needed a team for what He had to do. He knew that they needed to be diverse; He did not choose all of the same types of men. He understood that there would be a need for a John who was more relational, gentler, and less abrasive than Peter. But their diversity was designed for their functions. In order for them to unlock their diverse strength, they had to have unity. The whole purpose is destroyed in many relationships as well as churches. It is destroyed when you have some John trying to make everyone feel and act like him. Or some strong-willed Peter who doesn't know that he doesn't need everyone on his staff or his team to be just like him. The power wasn't really released in these men until these very different men came to Pentecost and got the same spirit. Different men though they were, their forces unfolded when they got in the same directional wind and began to flow together. Jesus knew the power of partnerships based on diversity, a common direction, and a deliberate destination.

Is your life filled with diverse people who are committed to a common goal? Have you surrounded yourself with a team of traveling companions who include as one of their priorities your well-being? Do your relationships raise you up and along the road to success? When you assess your relationships, prune the ones that are not fruitful, and nurture the ones that are bountiful. Then you will be well on your way to maximizing some of the sweetest moments of your life!

THREE

—◆—

LOSING TO WIN

No matter who we or how long we live, the harsh reality of mortal life means that our time here on earth will always seem too short, too fleeting. The Psalmist reminds us of the fragile beauty of our lives when he writes, "As for man, his days are like grass; as a flower of the field, so he flourishes. For the wind passes over it, and it is gone, and its place remembers it no more" (Psalm 103:15–16, NKJV). This image reminds me of watching a field of dandelions set free by the soft summer breath of the wind on a balmy afternoon. One moment the field billows with the pale white cotton-ball blooms. The next moment, whoosh, and the wind sweeps them away. We are only here for a short time.

This harsh reality of our physical body's impermanence shocks the mind and stretches the soul of old and young alike. From the intellectual to the illiterate, death extends its universal power over each and every one of us. Regardless of race, creed, or color, we will all look death in the face and leave this existence. The awareness of our eventual death lingers like a shadow always alongside us even as we journey through the many seasons of life. As we walk along our path, we will experience joy and sorrow, challenge and change. We will walk beneath blue skies and bright sunshine; we will walk through the cascading torrents of rain, and the whistling wind of winter's cold chill. We will walk and walk until we grow weary and can walk no more, and all too soon the journey comes to an end.

Our time in this life is very short, indeed. In light of this, the time we do have becomes very precious—every hour seems vital, every second should be lovingly savored. Recognizing what a valuable commodity time is affects our approach to life, love, and even business. *Every moment that you live is an irreplaceable resource with a limited supply.* No matter how important, beautiful, wealthy, or powerful you may be, time waits on no one.

Don't get me wrong—it's not that I believe that this life is the main course. I believe in eternal life and that death is only a birth canal to a life greater than anyone here has ever seen. But while I wait for the great ascension up the "crystal stairs"—as Langston Hughes, the African American writer, so aptly describes the transition from this life into the next—I must be the best steward of the time I'm given.

Life is an irrevocable trust. You take it as it comes, and through wise use of your time, you can avoid repeating old mistakes. Although no one can change their past, thank God you can leave it all behind. You and I must maximize each day. We must do this not because this life is all we have. No, we maximize the moments of this life as a runner runs his race, knowing that this particular race cannot and will not ever be repeated in quite the same way again. Regardless of what will come next, this race will not be run again. So I must embrace this race and make the most of time to reach my destination. I must cast my past cares to the wind and stretch my sweat-drenched legs into the stride of a young roe and run without looking back to see what was left behind. Nor can I have anxiety about the next lap's turning. I must run with the next step in mind and that step alone. It is that step that I cannot afford to miss. If I trip there, I may fall and never get up. You see, these are our laps to run, and they will soon be behind us rather than before. So today we must run with the awareness that each lap, in fact each step, does count.

Do you not know that those who run in a race all run, but one receives the prize? Run in such a way that you may obtain it. (1 Corinthians 9:24, NKJV)

ATTIC FANATIC

Knowing that we must make each step of each lap count, why, then, would we allow ourselves to carry weight that might affect the success of our flight through this brief moment of time? Why would we not inspect what we will be concerned with and what we will ignore? Why would we spend these days tangled in a web of petty problems and meaningless matters? While some trials and turmoils have a pitch and volume that cannot be turned down or ignored, others are merely annoying vibrations that can be diminished with the flick of a switch. It is to them that I now turn my attention.

As sure as I am in this world, most of us endure the weight and worry of countless things that older and wiser people will tell you have no real importance. And we spend the limited resources of our energies extinguishing fires that would burn out on their own, often within days or minutes, if left alone. The greatest threat we face is the threat of wasted time. Ravenous seconds have insatiable appetites, threatening to eat our life like cannibals in the jungle and leave the cleanly chewed bones of regret behind for us to behold as age paints its wrinkled brush across our brow. *Never forget that time is your most limited resource.* Save your time and you have increased your assets and decreased your liabilities.

In order to utilize this precious commodity of time and achieve your full potential, you must learn to lose the weight of the world, the cloying relationships and obligations that cling to you like second-hand smoke, poisoning the pure air you need to survive and thrive. In order to win, you must first lose. Lose the baggage of old relationships, pointless fears, and false indebtedness from manipulators in your life. There are enough hard circumstances and painful trials in life that we must endure; why endure ones that we can lay aside? Realizing, then, that many anguished moments cannot be avoided, why would we complicate the race by refusing to remove what we can from our shoulders? When Blind Bartimaeus heard that Jesus was passing by, he threw aside his coat (Mark 10:46–52). Likewise, there are some things you must disengage from if you are going to run and run well.

> Therefore we also, since we are surrounded by so great a cloud of witnesses, let us lay aside every weight, and the sin which so easily ensnares us, and let us run with endurance the race that is set before us. (Hebrews 12:1, NKJV)

As an athlete in training can tell you, you must learn to limit your diet in order to get rid of the weight that hinders your performance. I call this the Weight of the World diet—laying aside the pounds of chains that restrain you from the maximum use of the time you are given. You need to dismiss the "fatty" issues from your life. You need to cut out the junk that bloats you up and weights you down. You must strive to eliminate those things that fill your life but offer nothing to nourish you.

If you want to have some semblance of peace, ask God for the grace to determine what to keep in your life and what to eliminate. It is not always easy to discern between the two without looking through the keen lenses of wisdom with microscopic clarity. What energizes, enlivens, and enables your performance as a runner? And what drains, depletes, and destroys?

It reminds me of some grandmas' attics. If you have ever had to go in the house of some sweet little grandma and clean out the attic, you will notice that in most cases what started out in only one corner of the attic has grown over the years until the floor starts sagging, causing the ceilings of the rooms below to sag as well. In extreme cases, for a grandma who's an attic fanatic, the top room may be so weighted down with old, useless junk that it jeopardizes the rest of the house. Look in many grandmas' attics and you'll find broken furniture, old-fashioned clothing with moth holes and mildew, cracked baby pictures, old toys from the first Christmas in the new house. The place is cluttered with her first sewing machine that Henry bought her, the one with the pedal at the bottom. Then there is that washing machine with the wringer at the top that used to pinch her hands when she fed wet sheets through it. None of these items and the hundreds of others are any good today: She just can't bring herself to get rid of anything. In fact, the closets all over the house are filled with old items. She has kept everything. She even brags about how much she has kept. But what grandma doesn't re-alize or won't accept is that some things—no matter how wonderful they were at one time—must go. They do not work anymore, they serve no function, and they are a fire hazard and a death trap. She lacks the courage to let things go.

As terrible as that is, grandma is not alone. Most of us hold onto the familiar even when it isn't working anymore. We keep old dead rela-tionships, sentimental about people who are not sentimental about us. We remain loyal to a company that is not loyal to us. We religiously use brand-name products without even considering trying new or improved ones. Most of us drive the same way home every day. Our lives are so rit-ualized that we never consider any options at all. Today you must real-ize that you have options. You do not have much time; life is short. How you spend it is up to you. You have options at your disposal, but you cannot pick up anything with your hands full. You have to make choices. All of us get something, but none of us gets it all. Every give-me has a got-you. No matter what decisions you make, there will be assets and li-abilities. Compare the assets to the liabilities and then choose.

The choice is yours. Decide what you will allow to cling to your soul and what you will strip away. It is your soul that must remain buoyant in life if you are going to be as creative and effective as you can. This is an exercise in choices and priorities. One has to choose what one is going to carry, because there are some things that must be carried. There are some troubles that you must make room for and others that are needless clutter left laying on the floor in the life of someone who will not make decisions, develop priorities, or bring closure.

FACING THE FEARS

Why would anyone cling to the useless clutter of their life rather than drop the weight and run more freely? The answer is simple, and it's something that we all must face and stare down: fear. Franklin D. Roosevelt, in his first inaugural address, declared, "Let me assert my firm belief that the only thing we have to fear is fear itself—nameless, unreasoning, unjustified terror which paralyzes needed efforts to convert retreat into advance." Spoken at the height of the Great Depression, his statement is nonetheless appropriate for us today. Fear cripples creativity and diminishes self-image. Fear creeps into your life, often leaving you impotent to perform.

One of the greatest fears men and women face is the fear of failure, the fear that we will not "make it," the nagging insecurity that we won't succeed or be good enough. Too often we forget that we are always "good enough" in the eyes of the Lord. We are all His children, we are His Creation, and as such we are a success.

But still there are moments in which fear screams so loudly in your ears that you think, "There's no way I'm going to make it." The first time your mouth says it or your mind thinks it, you have dented your armor and undermined your effectiveness. If you let it fester in you, it will infect you like a plague and demolish your creativity all together.

Life will give you enough real enemies to fight without fighting the ghosts and goblins, the haunting voices that lurk in the shadows of your mind. It is not a tragedy to lose a race when you know you have done your best. The challenge comes when you finish third, with your cheeks flushed and your lungs ablaze, and you have to hear the nagging voice in your head that whispers that you could have run it more effectively if you had only done this or that. Regret is the murderer of optimism and the evangelist of despair. It breeds in dark places like mold on crusted bread.

Who wants to get up in the morning and look into a face that sneers back and says, "You could have run further, but you wouldn't strip for the race"? That's right, I said strip. Drop everything that is not essential so that you can run faster, soar higher, and reach further and achieve your full potential.

Fear must be at the top of the list of things that you must strip off. In fact, let's start a grocery list of items we will *not* be bringing home with us anymore. The first thing we will leave behind us is fear. It is the enemy of greatness, the opposite of faith. The longer it lives within you, the stronger it lives within you. Fear is fertilized by words. But it is not the words that others say that leave you trembling or intimidated. No, it is the words that you say to yourself. Now, I better make this clear because many of you are not likely to sit in the corner literally trembling. You will pass over this section as if it doesn't apply to you unless I identify the fact that all fear doesn't manifest itself in the kind of trembling that is obvious. Some fears that rob you and weight you down manifest themselves in pettiness and jealousy. Some fears manifest in your need to make people know who you are and what you have done because you secretly fear that you will be overlooked or not measure up to the mark.

Fear is what causes men to feel insulted by women who make more money than they do. It is not always the trembling neurotic fear that makes us bite our fingernails that has to be fought. It is the fear that will affect your character and cause you to do devious things in order to climb ladders that are not even worth the trip. These are weights that hinder you from having good success. There is a difference between success and good success. Good success adds no sorrow to it. But success alone can make you miserable.

> *This Book of the Law shall not depart from your mouth, but you shall meditate in it day and night, that you may observe to do according to all that is written in it. For then you will make your way prosperous, and then you will have good success.*
>
> *Have I not commanded you? Be strong and of good courage; do not be afraid, nor be dismayed, for the LORD your God is with you wherever you go. (Joshua 1:8–9, NKJV)*
>
> *The blessing of the LORD makes one rich, and He adds no sorrow with it. (Proverbs 10:22, NKJV)*

To strip yourself of the enemy of fear, you must first identify it. Fear will hide in your motives. It will drape itself in overprotectiveness and anger, but it is a liar hiding in your motives. It will feed your mind with clutter and weigh you down with the responsibility of feeling like you have to look out for yourself, protect yourself, and defend yourself. Fear inflates itself so much that it may make you forget that there is Someone greater than the self, and He is looking out for you. Fear is an added weight you do not need. Remember, the worst enemies to fight are the ones that live within.

Ask yourself every day: How can I maximize my life if I do not minimize my baggage? The excessive baggage of fear will defeat you every time. Airplanes will not fly without checking the weight load. No one flies high with too much weight. The higher you fly, the less dead weight you can carry. Stop listening to the words of fear trying to cut you from within. Stay focused on the prize, not on the threats of harsh competitors. Most of all, learn to the hear the Master's voice whispering your true identity. Like the most beloved coach who desires and empowers our ultimate victory, our God speaks to us if we will only listen. We must stare down the fears, both within and without. In order to maximize the moment, you must ask yourself, "What is the best use of my time?" You must address when to say hello and when to say goodbye to old issues that threaten to make you stagnant. You must realize what you are truly afraid of and exercise the courage to let it go so that you may run like the hart across the mountainside.

BURNING THE MORTGAGE

After releasing our fears, the second thing we must strip off is old debt. I do not mean debt in the traditional sense of bills and financial encumbrances, though that is certainly worth avoiding. No, today we are trying to make sure that you strip off the debt that people leave on your door step because they helped you or were "there for you" at one time or another. Appreciate everyone, honor them, and help whoever you can, but avoid allowing people to leave you with a feeling of eternal indebtedness to them. This "I am forever grateful to you" syndrome sounds noble, but it actually robs God of His glory. It suggests that you are where you are because of who He used. The reality is simple. First, promotion comes only from God. Second, if He uses someone to open the door, you must realize that it is your gift that makes it stay open. Like a comedian who gets to the stage, once you are on, it is up to you and the level of your ability to entertain the audience. Indebtedness will weigh you down and often requires that you have long strings attached to people who take credit for what God has done in your life.

Whenever possible, pay your own way. When someone is a blessing to you, recognize them but watch out for leaches that will overtax you and leave you in debt the rest of your life. At some point, you have to decide enough is enough.

> *Give everyone what you owe him: If you owe taxes, pay taxes; if revenue, then revenue; if respect, then respect; if honor, then honor. Let no debt remain outstanding, except the continuing debt to love one another, for he who loves his fellowman has fulfilled the law. (Romans 13:7–8, NIV)*

As we can see from Paul's letter to the church at Rome, we are to pay our own way as much as we can so that we are free from petty debts and bitter resentments in order to love each other better. Love is the one debt that can never be paid in full. The problem comes when we allow others to manipulate our feelings of gratitude into an ongoing debt, which belongs only to love.

This presumption of indebtedness is the sin of Gehazi, a servant of Elisha, who couldn't stand to see the Aramean leader Naaman receive his healing without recompense. He was convinced that he should receive more than was due him. In so doing he brought down destruction upon himself. Sadly, he didn't realize that it wasn't he who had healed Naaman but God. His incessant greed caused him to die with the leprosy that God had lifted from Naaman.

> *But Elisha said to him, "Was not my spirit with you when the man got down from his chariot to meet you? Is this the time to take money, or to accept clothes, olive groves, vineyards, flocks, herds, or menservants and maidservants? Naaman's leprosy will cling to you and to your descendants forever." Then Gehazi went from Elisha's presence and he was leprous, as white as snow. (2 Kings 5:26–27)*

We all have people who have blessed us in ways that we will never forget. We honor them and we appreciate them, as well we should. But there will always be a few who want more than they are due. These will fall into the Gehazi category and destroy themselves with their insatiable thirst for more and more compensation. People who want more than their fair share of credit bring destruction on themselves, and they will leave you depleted if you try to feed their lust for recognition and greed. It reminds me of the mortgage-burning parties our grandparents and parents used to have when the old home was finally paid off. They would take a copy of the document of indebtedness, which was now marked "Paid in Full," and light a match to the crisp parchment. Neighbors, friends, and family members would celebrate this wondrous occasion with singing and a potluck supper as the charred paper went up in smoke. The debt had been paid, the obligation was no longer due. However, the Gehazis of the world show up at the door and still try to collect a mortgage that had been paid in full. Because there was once a debt, or because there was once an obligation, these people cannot accept that we have burned our mortgage papers and moved on in our lives. We must release the ashes of our burned mortgages to the wind, no longer bound by the callous collectors hounding us for more.

Unfortunately, these hangers-on can be hard to shake. They want to fly when they see you going higher. But you have to know that, as your altitude increases, you have to make hard choices about what goes with you along the way. It is great to be a nice person, but you must know that being nice does not always mean that you are fulfilling your purpose and maximizing your time to its fullest potential. You can be a nice person who settles for mediocrity because of the weight of obligation. It would be absurd to continue to make monthly payments to the bank on a mortgage that was paid off long ago. Putting niceness above our own well-being is folly.

WEIGHT WATCHERS

How do we begin to sort through our relationships and relinquish the hindrances that cling to us like briars on our clothes? We must make hard choices, keeping the end goal in mind, not the temporary discomfort of the work at hand. There are times when we need to learn and develop ways to say goodbye. Here are some simple guidelines to help you confront the relationships that weigh you down. By acknowledging them and reacquainting ourselves with our true goals, we can lose the unwanted weight and keep it off. We must commit ourselves to getting into the best shape for maximizing and maintaining our moments.

1. Accept disappointing realities.

Self-deceit is the enemy of greatness. You have to admit to yourself that certain relationships are not working. You have to realize that your efforts to rehabilitate this person or that have failed. If you are a chronically caped crusader, like I am, you may have this fierce need to help the victim or underdog. But you cannot help everyone. Sometimes you have to accept the fact that your efforts are not enough. Swallow your pride with a tall glass of realism and admit that these relationships are weighing you down. Releasing them doesn't mean that these people will never get better. It just means that God is better suited at this than you are. Release them to the One who never fails.

2. Do not try to be someone else's God.

Many times when you see the predicament of others, you want to help. Often you can. But be careful of people who seem to be in perpetual need and always turn to you. They are always calling your name and try to make you feel guilty for not always being there for them. But only God can always be there.

Keep in mind, too, that there is a difference between helping someone and carrying them. Making a loan to a friend is one thing and welfare is something else. Your constant help may even be a hindrance. You may think you're just being nice, but you may be becoming a crutch, an enabler. Why should they even try if you're always there to do everything for them?

Sure, helping others makes you feel good, but your need to be needed is getting in the way of their need to grow. Step back and let others walk on their own. Often, people discover God when they are left alone. Stop being a god-player and let God tend to His flock.

3. Become comfortable with criticism.

When you know that you have done all that you could but determine that you must end a relationship, accept the fact that not everyone will be happy with you. No matter who you are, you cannot please everyone all of the time. Sometimes the fear of criticism will imprison your common sense. What will they think of me? What will they say about me? It is true that people do not accept terminations well. But this is a matter of your survival. You must realize that if you are going to reach the heights you have been called to reach, you may elicit some criticism from those who are jealous, petty, or angry because they were left behind.

> Woe to you when all men speak well of you, for that is how their fathers treated the false prophets. (Luke 6:26, NIV)

False prophets were well spoken of because they didn't speak truth. Truth sometimes hurts and it often alienates, but it is still the truth. There are times you just have to tell it like it really is and accept the consequences, knowing full well that some people will criticize you for it. The only way to avoid criticism is to always say what everyone wants to hear, but that makes you a false prophet. When someone keeps abusing your kindness and all you say, in both word and deed, is, "I don't mind. It's okay," you're not telling the truth. The truth is that it is not okay. You do mind. You are living a lie in the relationship. You are a false prophet. Yes, people are speaking well of you, but they are also stealing the life out of you and hindering your dream. Their compliments are far too costly. Let them speak ill of you. It is worth it to clean out your attic and lose the unneeded weight.

4. Develop a budget for each level of your relationships.

Every relationship works better for both people when the dimensions of that relationship are established from the first. You cannot maximize your life with foggy, cluttered relationships. Successful, productive people do not have time to spend their life straightening out constant misunderstandings, hurt feelings, and damaged egos.

If you want to keep the relationship low maintenance, I suggest that you develop the dimensions early, discuss the parameters clearly, and make sure that both of you are comfortable with the conclusions. Occasionally, as you grow, you will see things that require renegotiation. Do not be afraid to renegotiate the terms of the relationship if you are not getting what you need. Or if you are not being treated fairly, it is time to speak up.

How far are you willing to go and how much are you willing to invest in each of your relationships? Ultimately, you have control. Avoid relationships that drain you and leave you asking, "How did I get in to this?" You may have exceeded your budget emotionally, physically, or otherwise, or it may simply be because this person needs too much time to feel that you are close. They need too many phone calls, dinners, favors, loans, or other forms of attention. You see, you only have so much time. You only have so much energy. You have to be a good steward of your time and resources and spend them where there is the greatest return to you and to God. That return may only be the warm feeling of knowing that you helped someone. If that is what you want or need, that is fine. The bottom line is simple: You set the budget, not the other person. If too-needy people are holding out for more, and if they make you feel obligated to give, then you need to walk away. Going bankrupt yourself by making someone else feel great might sound noble, but it is not. Bankrupt people can end up with everything from nervous breakdowns to extramarital affairs. Don't overspend! Develop your budget and stick to it.

5. Compartmentalize the relationships you keep.

Compartmentalizing will salvage many important relationships. Sometimes some aspects of a relationship should be terminated and other areas should be maintained. It is possible to have relationships that work in one area but not in another. You do not have to throw away the baby with the bath water.

When you feel a relationship is not working, first step back. View the situation objectively instead of emotionally. Emotions may cause you to throw away everything even though there are many things about the relationship that you enjoy. By looking at facets of your relationship in a more objective way, you can then reassess where things stand and how you want to proceed. You cannot negotiate in a rage, so you must get a grip on your feelings. You would be surprised what a good open conversation will do when you openly confront someone and say, "This isn't working for me in its current form, but I want to maintain our relationship. There are so many things about you I really enjoy and need." Though they may initially feel despondent, most people respect the truth (people who don't respect truth are often the critics referred to in #3).

Compartmentalized relationships require that you see the relationships as slices of an orange. It is possible to remove this or that slice and still have a lot left to enjoy. It does take effort and communication, but it is often worth it. It means that there are some common interests that need to be maintained, but there are some others that need to be annulled before all its lost. You can't just let things go unchecked. Eventually, you must confront issues or you will waste your time and spend your life in a stalemate, locked in pent-up, silent frustration. Don't forget the three Ds of strong partnerships: diversity, direction, and a deliberate destination.

6. Progressively terminate dead relationships.

My grandmother used to say something to me when I was a child, which at the time made no sense at all. She said, "Boy, when you got your head in a lion's mouth, wiggle real easy until you get it out. Then knock his teeth out!" I never understood at seven years old what she meant, but I do now. You shouldn't just leave your head in there, but if you try to hit the lion while your head is in its mouth, chances are those sharp teeth are going to come down hard upon your head. My mom called it cutting off your nose to spite your face. No matter what you call it, don't do it.

Gradual separations are often the wisest solution. There are some relationships you just have to get out of, but just because you have a cord to cut doesn't mean that it has to be ripped. Dissolving relationships can be stressful for both parties. End them gradually. The cord that binds us may be the frequency of phone calls or visits. We can just gradually decrease them without finding it necessary to formally dissolve a relationship where there has been just a difference of direction but no conflict. Just remember, if you have your head in the lion's mouth, don't hit him just yet. It might be better to do a little gradual wiggling until you get your head out.

7. Never revisit what you have thoroughly examined before.

Many people are so nice that they cannot end a relationship and go forward. They just keep going back at every chance to reevaluate the decisions that they made. Make it once. Make it right. And make it final. Often people will come back around to entice you by suggesting that you were wrong the first time. But you should resolve any reasonable doubt before you make the decision in the first place. My wife often goes crazy waiting on me to make a decision. It takes me forever to give up on anyone or anything. I have to resolve all of the possible scenarios that might be tried to make things better. But once I finally have convinced myself that all options have been explored, I move on. Like justice, my wheels turn slow, but I grind very fine.

> *As a dog returns to his own vomit, so a fool repeats his folly. (Proverbs 26:11, NKJV)*

An unpleasant image, but it is so true. Too often, people keep repeating the same patterns over and over again. In order to maximize your life, you need to become more time-conscious and realize that you cannot afford to lose time by needless repeats.

LOSE TO WIN

So right now if you have a life that looks like a garage, filled with debris and clutter, you must take inventory. Maybe you are ready to move forward, but you have so much weight and garbage collected that you are being weighted down and you are losing the joy of your life, the productivity of your associations, and the peace of your friendships. Life is too short. Get a grip. That is a modern way of saying gain control. It is not control of the other person; you don't want to be perceived as a manipulator. But get control over your own life and stop allowing other people's feelings to manipulate your decisions.

There are times, so I've learned the hard way, that helping people will hurt you. In fact, helping them can kill you if you do not know when to say enough is enough. It's comparable to enjoying food so much that you overeat until there's too much girth to swiftly run the race to the best of your ability. When you gain too much weight, obesity takes a toll on your entire body—heart, blood pressure, nervous system, and lungs. We must lose the weight and train to run the race with speed and endurance. We must assess what we can do without in order to maximize what we have been given. Ultimately, we must lose to win!

FOUR

———

INTERLUDES
OF SILENCE

A weary traveler trudges along his way. His feet hurt and his legs are weak. His vision has grown strained, his eyes have begun to see the road as one big blurred haze. There is nothing like tiredness to dull the senses and lull the mind into a catatonic state. Exhaustion leads to carelessness and confusion. If the traveler is wise, he or she will pause for a moment, recognizing that the time delayed is far better than the trip aborted by disaster. Even a quick rest will break the monotony of the trek and restore energy.

Like the weary traveler's long, winding road, life also has a tendency to dull the senses, numb the brain, and stiffen the joints. If we do not back up from our task from time to time and spend a moment enjoying something other than the challenge of day-to-day living, we will see everything blurred, and the bright colors of life will turn into one generic shade of gray. The value of rest cannot be calculated by fiscal-year statements, budget reports, charts, or graphs. It will not show up as an asset on your year-end tax statement. But the bottom line is still effective. If you want to have the greatest impact when you do work, then you need to take a recess with a Sabbath for the soul.

STILL THE MOMENT

Every so often even a deer breaks his gait and rests, allowing his heaving chest a moment to pant its way into a calm and gracious moment of solitude. Gleeful birds occasionally hush their whistling chatter in order to soak in the awesome tonic of absolute silence. Often your ears will ache for the sweet sound of nothingness. It is in this quiet calm of solitude that our passion to live is rekindled. Everything in nature needs to be revived from time to time. It is to this end that the winter gives the soil a rest after the harvest season. The cold blight that covers the grassy meadow allows the weary ground a chance to rejuvenate itself.

In the same sense, creativity drains the human soul like a harvest depletes rich soil. If the depleted soil needs a time of rest to replenish what it has given, how much more the human soul. Quite often, men and women who are productive maintain a feverish pitch of striving. They often are not aware that there is an erosion that occurs in the human soul from ordinary wear and tear. This erosion causes us to feel tired in a way that defies sleep. We sleep but find no rest, because we are weary in more than our bodies. Some call it burnout, others refer to is as a breakdown. I call it the weariness of the soul. I know you do not think that it can happen to you, but it can. Worse still, you can burn out and not have the benefit of a diagnosis. Many times we burn out, and it produces symptoms that we think are irrational. These include anger, irritable behavior, rash decisions, disenchantment, and low morale on the job. We tend to blame others for our lack of passion for work or marriage, never once thinking that maybe the blame belongs to ourselves. We have been walking too long and working too hard, and we haven't stopped to take a rest. We need to still the moment and restore ourselves. We need to respect our soul's need to be replenished. If we want to be productive, effective, and reach our full potential, every once in a while we need to take a break.

It seems strange that someone who is a capable of managing a large firm or developing complex budgets may not have the common sense to know that they are tired and need to rest. Yet, the lives of great men and women are often pitched loud and paced fast. Their gait is often at breakneck speed. They are driven to perform, produce, and please. Yes, they are successful, but their days are filled with endless tasks and their nights are riddled with thought of what else needs to be done. They are constantly on the go, always doing, always thinking.

It is true that one must work hard in order to succeed. We must be focused and persevere at the task at hand so that we may reach our goals. But the truly wise, the truly great, know that you must utilize your resources but not deplete them. Well-timed rest restores your energy and maintains your abilities so that you can function to your full capacity. Too much work, too much stress, being pulled in too many directions, will erode your soul and undermine all your efforts. Periodic pit stops will keep you running at peak performance.

MAINTENANCE MATTERS

Why do so many people run themselves into the ground? How can we ignore our own needs so much? Is it that we are not aware of our soul's need for rest? Or, more likely, is it that we do not listen to the telltale signs of burnout? It is like a driver who drives a car but never listens to its engine. He's so concerned about where he's going and how fast he can get there that he doesn't notice that the engine is knocking, the tires are losing air, and the gas tank is almost empty. Before long, the car breaks down, stalled at the side of the road while everybody else passes by. The driver could have avoided the breakdown if only he had paid attention to his vehicle, listened to the noises, felt how the car handled. But instead, he waited until the car wouldn't move before he noticed that something was wrong. He should have heeded the signs.

You are like a car whose mileage now warrants that it be brought in for a diagnostic analysis and a complete checkup. The checkup should not be postponed until there is a clamoring knock under the hood or a dead engine. It should not be ignored until the car is stalled on some major interstate with smoke billowing out of it. All too late, the owner acknowledges that he or she has ignored the warning signs and failed to take the time to prevent possible calamities by maintaining the car on a regular basis. In the same way, we often ignore the warning signs, misappropriate our priorities, and contribute to our own calamities. We find ourselves stalled emotionally, spiritually, physically, and/or relationally primarily because we failed to rest, nurture, and rejuvenate ourselves.

Listen to your inner voice. It's not a spooky, eerie, "twilight zone" voice. It's just that normal mood-swinging, bored, indifferent hum that develops in the midst of busyness, the lethargy that indicates that you're burning the candle at both ends and soon the wick will be gone and the light will go out. The light in your eyes will flicker and go out if you do not take time for your soul.

It is foolish to wait until some moral or emotional failure occurs before you stop to analyze the who, what, when, where, and whys of your life. When a thirst or a need is not attended to, it will find relief some way. Have you ever tried to submerge a beach ball in a swimming pool? Even if you take it to the bottom of the deep end, it will buoy back to the surface—it will not stay hidden beneath the placid waters. Like a parched beast, the needy person will stalk, anxiously searching for fulfillment. If she finds no brook in a conventional, appropriate place, she will seek the dark drippings of a cave. There, draped in secrecy, the weary pilgrim, her rational mind eclipsed by exhaustion, licks the cold rocks of a sin-ridden cave desperate for relief and gratification. She herself doesn't realize what has driven her to such a desperate measure or why she finds it hard to break away.

After disaster has aborted her mission and robbed her of her chance at victory, she sadly reflects on her dilemma, trying to determine what happened to subvert the success she seemed destined to attain. How is it that the mighty fall? How is it that the carpenter's home lay in shambles? Could it be that we fail to maintain the greatness that we aspire so desperately to attain because we do not tend to ourselves with the same respect that we give our work? We must remember that the agile mind, functioning with adroitness and precision, is often just the result of a good night's rest. How can we perform well without a reprieve? In short, getting the best out of yourself requires the development of a healthy respect for rest.

No journalist writes her story at the scene of the crime. Isn't it true that creativity springs higher in the calm, tranquil moments of repose when the excitement smolders and the shrill sirens have hushed into the night? It is in the silence of the moments after the event that we gather our thoughts, rehash our observations, and organize the strategy for delivering the abstract dimensions of the moments we beheld. The reflective silence of a later time is the birthing table from which great work is born. It is that same table where the architect sketches his blueprint. It is in the darkroom that the picture develops. No picture of worth is developed on first sight. It requires a dark, quiet place for us to get the deep, rich color and sharp image. Yet most of us are as washed out as an underdeveloped picture. We have rushed the process, ruined the negatives, and routed our potential, all because we seek to do too much too fast.

DEVELOP THE REAL YOU

Often we will not confide to others with transparent honesty who we are inside. Certain people pride themselves on being in control. They show others only what they want others to see. They maintain a mask that they display to the world. They always seem to have it together. These controllers seem invincible, able to do anything, able to be anything. But the truth is that no one is invincible. There is only One who is Everything. All the rest of us are human. And when Ms. In Control realizes that she is human, she often will hide in the shadows, confused and afraid. She fears that if anyone knew that she was human or vulnerable, they would not respect her. Also, and more important, she often feels disappointed in herself. She and others like her do not realize that the distraught heart of an overworked mind drives the desperation. They work so hard at doing it all and doing it perfectly, and the moment they slip even the tiniest bit, they fall into a pit of despair, hiding out of shame and beating themselves up. Instead of going for help, they generally add more fuel to the fire, more work to their already heavy load. What was already ablaze with stress then becomes a blazing inferno until the fire fizzles out and our dreams, our hopes, even our will to keep going, are extinguished.

As I mentioned before, we are like a car that needs a service check periodically. Some of you may think it is ridiculous to go through all the trouble to bring a car in for a checkup when it seems to be running fine. You rationalize, "I must be okay; I am still running." But if you want to run fine for a long time, you will need to have some time and a place in your life where you steal away and look up under the hood. The paint may not be peeling, the mag wheels may look great, and the bucket seats may be polished. But stress hides under the hood and clogs the engine with residual gunk. Rest allows us to check under the hood.

> *The heart is deceitful above all things, and desperately wicked: who can know it?*
> *(Jeremiah 17:9, KJV)*

Unfortunately, many of us deceive ourselves, not admitting when we need a break. Knowing yourself is a major accomplishment. Knowing yourself well enough to know when to say "when" can save your life. Self-deceit is common amongst those who esteem the work that they perform as more important than the worker who performs it. I call it the Martyr Syndrome. It is amazing how often we die for a cause, sabotaging our true greatness.

Instead, we must allow our false pride to die in order to be our best. You must know we all need a place to rest for a moment, to rethink where we are and refuel for the journey ahead. Facing the future without rest is like trying to drive the car with the fuel gauge on "E." We find ourselves depleted and ill-prepared for the journey before us, and we fail not for the lack of desire or giftedness, but only from the lack of rest. The Psalmist was well aware of how disturbed we become when we do not attend to our soul's care.

> *These things I remember as I pour out my soul: how I used to go with the multi-*
> *tude, leading the procession to the house of God, with shouts of joy and thanksgiv-*
> *ing among the festive throng. Why are you downcast, O my soul? Why so disturbed*
> *within me? (Psalm 42:4–5, NIV)*

Have you ever asked yourself the question, "What is wrong with me?" Maybe you don't talk to yourself, but perhaps you should. Maybe you should take the time to ask yourself questions and get answers. These are the questions whose answers often reveal the collected crud that clings like barnacles to the souls of busy people. These questions bring to light the stress polluting your body, mind, and soul. Left undetected, it will produce depression and discomfort even in the midst of success. It is astonishing that you could have a bad time at a good moment in your life. Nevertheless, it is still true.

In his novel *A Tale of Two Cities,* Charles Dickens recognized this striking paradox. He writes, "It was the best of times and the worst of times." You might ask, "How can that be possible? How can things be going their very best and also be at their very worst?" If you don't know now, keep living and you will. The reality is simple. A great moment comes at the end of hard work. No one encounters sustained success without massive strain and challenge. The stress, left unchecked, will rob you of the feeling of accomplishment. The pressure that builds within us often creeps up the back stairs and burglarizes our feelings of satisfaction. We are left insatiable and needy for something that tangibles cannot provide. Only rest will defuse the time bomb that stress creates. Only when you stop can you fully appreciate your accomplishments.

You must evaluate your success-stress-rest process to ensure that you are guarding your soul and protecting your heart. Here are a few ways for you to readily determine if you are losing your momentum or your enthusiasm. Think through or, better yet, write down your yes or no answers to these questions as honestly and thoughtfully as you can.

1. Are you often sullen and disgruntled when you are away from work? What do you think causes these feelings?
2. Does your life seem one-dimensional because there is little if any diversity in your lifestyle? What are you looking forward to in the coming week?
3. Do you wake up in the morning feeling tired and drained? Is it hard to drag yourself out of bed?

4. Are you losing your passion, sense of humor, or optimism?
5. Do you jump from one goal to another without stopping to appreciate what you have already attained?
6. Do you ever find yourself unexpectedly crying or inwardly hopeless?
7. Do you define yourself according to what you do rather than who you are?
8. Are you lowering your standards and losing your enthusiasm in areas where you were once meticulously detailed?
9. Do you find yourself wringing your hands and clenching your jaw, overwhelmed by problems that seem difficult to sort through?
10. Is your public demeanor devouring your private life?

If you answered yes to seven or more of these questions, then congratulations—you are the grand prize winner of a blue ribbon for burnout. The stress and demands of producing often leave you feeling depleted and dangerously empty. I know, I have been there. I am well aware of the many challenges that face people who are loaded with responsibility. The operative word here must be *balance.* Without balance, we lose our equilibrium and often fall headfirst into a pond of trouble that can range from immorality, which is often the desperate groping of the soul, to physical disorders and infirmities. Just think that all of this may result from the lack of some plain old rest.

REWARDS OF REST

Imagine a woman who has just birthed a child. The child may be a long-awaited answer to prayer. She now holds that miracle in her hands and smiles at the baby with a look of love and adoration. However, all of this joy does not stop her from having what doctors call postpartum blues. She can vacillate between happiness and dark depression. She has her baby, but she feels empty and depleted. For her, it is the best of times and the worst of times. The pregnancy is successfully ended, and yet she misses the previous stage when she carried a life within her. She feels drained emotionally and physically. She often doesn't understand her own feelings. She is exhausted. She has been successful, but she is still empty.

Like the new mother who has attained her goal but feels less exuberant than expected, we often are shocked to find that those goals we worked hard to attain do not always bring us the emotional fulfillment that we desired. It is just a phase, but it can seem like an eternity. Treat it with rest, bathe it with prayer, and watch your sensation of pleasure return like sea gulls to a beach after the storm has passed. We must allow ourselves the reward of rest in order to continue a productive journey.

Years ago when my wife and I were dating, I worked swing shift at a chemical plant. I remember coming home and calling her in the middle of the night. The phone would wake her from a restful sleep, and I would pour out my troubles to her. She would let me talk on and on, for she knew that when I was tired, I had the tendency to feel overwhelmed and depressed about a problem that I would not be disturbed about at all by the next morning. I am grateful for her patience with me, her willingness to listen, and her wise counsel to never make rash decisions. I have now learned that a little rest changes your perspective on the issue. Further, I realize that when you are tired, it is not wise to make decisions. It is during that time that a mood or a dark place in your soul can easily manipulate your judgment. I guess it is no different from a traveler who has been journeying too long down the highway. He may be an excellent driver, but his skills diminish with weariness so that he finds himself not performing at his peak. A simple thing like some rest, a change of scenery, a brief walk around the car will renew his spirit and enable him to proceed effectively.

Rest doesn't have to be a two-week, all-expenses-paid trip to the Bahamas. Many people wait on the big trips and lose the opportunity to have mini-excursions. Simple, little things can rest your soul, like eating in the park and lying on the grass rather than sitting in the same dim cubbyhole at work. It doesn't always have to be expensive, extravagant, or lavish to be restful. While you are waiting on the "big one," why not slip away by having your coffee on the roof of your apartment building early in the morning? For me, reading enables me to escape my life and the demands of others. It allows my soul the chance to throw open a window and ventilate my life with the fresh experiences of some enjoyable character—a medieval prince, perhaps—with a life very different from my own. You may find a need to take a break from the stress-laden, always-available, work-ridden person that you normally are and transform from a bustling butterfly into a slow-moving silkworm. This metamorphosis, though a step down, allows your wings to rest and your mind to play.

Finding an escape through a healthy mini-excursion doesn't mean that you don't like your life. It doesn't mean that you don't enjoy being who you really are. It doesn't mean that you want to alter your course. But like the driver who has spent too many hours glued to the interstate, we must often choose the scenic route just to break up the monotony of the journey. Taking a scenic route doesn't mean that the traveler doesn't want to go in the same direction; he just needs to enjoy the journey a bit more. The scenic route might be a little out of the way, it might take a little longer, but chances are he's more likely to stay on course and be happier along the way.

WAIT OF THE WORLD

Take a break and restore yourself. Walk down an unfamiliar street during your lunch hour. Instead of going straight home from work, stop at a bookstore and browse around. Or, best yet, find a quiet place to pray. The world can wait for an hour. It can wait because, believe it or not, it will go on without you. This realization can cause some folks to panic, to scurry even faster. In order to sustain ourselves, though, we must realize that since the world will race along without us, we must find our own pace and make our journey our own and not the world's.

Sadly, most of us do not take breaks, which would enable us to maximize and refuel our creativity. Many times we are ensnared by guilt, as if stopping would be irresponsible. Or we fear that we may be losing ground because we took a minute for ourselves. But remember, no matter how wonderful something may be, you still need a break sometimes. Women who raise their children at home may love them madly, but they still need occasional breaks from them. They need a break to spend time with their mate, to feel like a woman, rather than just someone's nanny. These mothers need some quality time alone with their mates, refueling the part of themselves that is almost parched from giving so much to their children and others. In fact, they may occasionally need a break from their husband, depending on how constrained their lives have been. Always remember that your teeth will bite your tongue if they are locked up too close too long! Don't misunderstand me: I am certainly not suggesting an affair. No, let's focus on something with positive consequences, something pleasing to God. It may be a few days spent at a health spa or a weekend away at her mother's. Is there no money in your budget for an excursion or a vacation? How about joining a gym downtown just to get away for quality time with your wonderful self? If not that, then consider a visit to a park, beach, museum, or art gallery.

A few days ago, my wife and I had a brief moment that allowed us to get away from our five children, the demanding pace, and all the household duties. She was about to cook dinner and settle down to the humdrum routine that was starting to choke us both. I said, "Let's go out to eat!" She replied, "Right now?" I said, "Yes, why not?" There was someone with the children and we had no demands that evening. We jumped up and dressed quickly, and as I backed the car out of the garage, I couldn't help but feel like we were escaping from Alcatraz! The whole evening we kept doting all over each other and smiling whimsically; we had spiced up a moment with some relaxation for our souls. We had escaped.

Our soul is escaped as a bird out of the snare of the fowlers: the snare is broken,
and we are escaped. (Psalm 124:7, KJV)

BRAKE AND BALANCE

One of the hardest things to achieve is not success but a sense of balance. Balance often eludes us as we focus on one thing at the expense of the other. I believe that the wise writer of Ecclesiastes said it best when he wrote that there is a time and a season for every purpose under heaven (Ecclesiastes 3:1–8). If that is true, what you and I want to achieve is the fine art of doing the right thing at the right time. We must recognize when to put the brakes on and restore balance. Like a heavy semi-truck driver with a load of precious cargo, we must realize that speeding down life's highway can cause the load to shift, to be imbalanced. We must slow down and rearrange the cargo in order to prevent disaster from a top-heavy rig.

True balance should be a ballast for the soul, a steady shifting of weight to meet the various priorities and responsibilities, so that we can take the next step on the tightrope. I have seen people who were resting when they should have been wrestling. I have also seen people who were wrestling when they should have been resting. Like Jacob who wrestled with an angel, we often wrestle with things we cannot change.

It took me years to realize that when I went to bed I should not go with half of my day wrapped around my head. I found myself as tired in the morning as I was when I went to bed that night. I slept all right, but I didn't rest. You see, all night long I wrestled with issues that couldn't be resolved until morning, anyway. I missed my time to rest, and I was affected in the morning. I can't tell you how many days I went to work feeling like the worn heel of an old shoe. I was less effective, more tense, and unable to perform to full capacity.

The Bible commands us not to worry. Jesus taught us that worry is one of the most ineffective pastimes that we acquire. Not one single hour is added to your life by worrying. We cannot talk about rest without confronting worry. Worry is often the assassin of rest. It stealthily stalks us and hijacks the mind. While we may continue to function publicly, there is still a sinister force lurking within us. This enemy called worry disorients moods, destroys creativity, and depletes the sense of completion, which comes from within and which cannot be achieved by the mere acquisition of things.

> *Therefore I tell you, do not worry about your life, what you will eat or drink; or about your body, what you will wear. Is not life more important than food, and the body more important than clothes? Look at the birds of the air; they do not sow or reap or store away in barns, and yet your heavenly Father feeds them. Are you not much more valuable than they? Who of you by worrying can add a single hour to his life? And why do you worry about clothes? See how the lilies of the field grow. They do not labor or spin. (Matthew 6:25–28, NIV)*

DO NOT DISTURB

And on the seventh day God ended His work which He had done, and He rested on the seventh day from all His work which He had done. (Genesis 2:2, NKJV)

Even God rested. If He did, then what about you? If the Creator of the Universe knows that even He must hang a Do Not Disturb sign on his door, then how much more should we reserve a moment for relaxation? When Johnny is a hard worker, he must make sure that he balances that work with an equal amount of pleasure and relaxation. When Jackie strives and drives herself to great accomplishment, she must take time to rest her self and regain her balance. Make sure you take time to smell the roses. Here are some tips for those whom God has blessed as hard workers but who struggle with the element of rest. Use them to hang out your own Do Not Disturb sign from time to time:

1. Don't allow others to control your stopwatch!

Take confident charge of your time and do not allow others to infringe on your commitment to rest and recovery. Take the time out you need when you need it. Refuse to be intimidated by the opinions of others. People have a tendency to feel qualified to know what you need. Only you know when it's time to say "when."

2. Recognize the need for rest in every season of your life.

Regardless of where you are in life, realize that every stage requires rest in order to successfully continue on to the next phase. Obviously, some seasons may allow for more rest than others; retirement is for people who worked hard. Nonetheless, we must realize the unique demands of each season (more about this in Chapter Ten) and find appropriate ways to rest our weary feet in order to walk the next mile on tomorrow's journey.

3. Work to fulfill your calling, not your falling.

Work can be an addiction. Do not use work like a narcotic. It is important that you know that work will not replace the lack of wholeness in your life. Work to accomplish the goals that you are called to, not the insatiable needs inside that only relationship with God and with others can bring. Avoid the addiction of workaholism so that you do not fall from overexertion, exhaustion, or overextension.

4. Work at resting.

If resting is difficult for you, don't try to do it all at once. Carry a certain amount of work with you and then wean yourself gradually away from it as the vacation nears. It may not be smart for you to come to a screeching halt after you have been fast-tracking your work life and then go to a deserted island where there is absolute silence. Ease into your rest slowly.

5. Reward yourself with rest.

Maximum effort without comparable reward will destroy the motivation to continue. Whether it is you, your children, or your employees, motivation is essential for massive production. In other words, if you work hard, you must play hard.

If we do not take the time to discover the interludes of silence, we will never maximize our moments' potential. It might seem that we only maximize ourselves when in motion, but the paradoxical truth is that maximizing who we are requires stillness and rest. Running without resting produces an athlete who will inevitably give up his journey due to fatigue, injury, or burnout. More important, the places of rest that we carve out for ourselves are often where we best assess our life, our dreams, our heartaches, our faith. The power of rest is that it allows us to enjoy the journey of life, not just the destination. The power of true soul Sabbath allows us to live out our destiny and discover God's glorious gifts.

Part Two

MASTER THE MOMENT

FIVE

⚊⚍⚏⚍⚊

MISSION CONTROL

My friend, most of us live life like fans at an NFL game. We stand on the edge of the playing field, observing the contenders. We stare and cheer, we boo and hiss, but it never occurs to us that we should be on the field. I am amazed when I listen to the speculation of couch-potato coaches who seem to know what ought to be done but never do it themselves. Unlike the NFL, which, though highly compensated, is basically a game, life is no game. It is a hard-hitting, no-holds-barred gladiator event, where only the strong survive. Life is not a tournament for the fearful but for the faithful. If we are going to win, we must realize that all that we have and hope for is at stake. To play with the aim to win, we must divorce ourselves from the tendency to live life from a reactive perspective. Many of us respond to life only after it hits us in the face. You will never maximize your life by merely reacting to whatever catastrophe happens each day. You must learn to rise above catastrophes, as they will always come, in order to make the most of your life and fulfill your life's destiny. How do you rise above them when they seem to hit us day after day relentlessly? It requires a deliberate strategy that puts you ahead of the game.

PLAN TO WIN

Do you have a life plan? Do you have a clear road map to reach the destination of your life's journey? If not, you have proven by your lack of action that you do not plan to win. Spiritual people have a tendency to think that walking by faith means that you have no plan. But since faith is defined as the substance of the things that you hope for, in Hebrews 11:1, then in order to have effective faith you must have a "thing that you hope for," or a goal. Now if you are going to set a goal, you will need a strategy to attain the goal, and it is faith that plays an integral part in developing that strategy. Faith is the fuel that generates a working strategy that gets you to your goal. The reality of the matter is that "faith without works is dead" (James 2:20, KJV).

No one wants to go to work without a plan. If you are going to build a house, you want an architectural design, a blueprint. If you are going to travel a distance by car, you want a reliable up-to-date map. If you are going to fly by plane, you want an itinerary. The plan is crucial to the results. Many well-meaning people get married without a plan. They raise children with no plan. They pastor churches with no plan. They work a job with no plan. If you ask them if they want to be successful, they'll look at you funny and say, "Of course!" But they never make specific plans to attain success, and then they wonder why they fail. It is because they wake up every morning with one goal: simply to get through that day. They feel so overwhelmed that they lose sight of the large canvas of their lives and get caught up in the frame. The clamor of the urgent drowns out the voice of the truly important. Consequently, these people stumble through each day without any consideration of their goals for that week, month, year, or season of their life. They succeed according to their short-sighted, limited plan.

If surviving the day is all you expect and plan for, that is all you are going to get!

On the other hand, long-term goals require an ongoing vision of success balanced with day-by-day details. True success necessitates dedication to a mission and the discipline, grace, and perseverance needed to live out that mission each and every day. For example, consider the wonders of our space program: the marvel of a rocket breaking through the earth's gravity and encircling our planet and returning safely; the wonder of a man walking on the moon, the incredible advent of space shuttles which fly to and from space with the grace and ease of a paper airplane sailing through the air on a spring day. These accomplishments did not just happen overnight. Someone did not show up at NASA one day and say, "I'd like to be an astronaut" or "Let's launch a rocket this afternoon." No, it took years and decades of patience, planning, and perseverance. It took a powerful crew of dedicated comrades collaborating together to ensure success. It took a ground crew committed to the same mission as the team of astronauts blasting through earth's atmosphere into the infinite black velvet of starlit space. The astronauts rely on the dedication of the mission control unit in order to succeed. Similarly, the men and women in the NASA control rooms see their dreams come to life in the steps their counterparts take into the great beyond. Both teams live out their commitment to a common mission on a daily basis.

It is the same for us. We must have a sense of mission control, a combination of a long-term visionary plan with the energy and action needed to accomplish it. If we are going to send the rockets of our dreams into orbit, then we must be committed to the mission. I recall a businessman who came to me recently asking my advice on a certain choice for his company. I asked him, "How does this opportunity fulfill your company's mission statement?" He looked at me sheepishly, then averted his eyes for a moment. "Do you know the ultimate mission for your business?" I asked gently. He shook his head and shrugged his shoulders.

"I guess to make a profit and survive another year." I replied, "Is that all? Don't you realize God wants you to do more than survive? He wants you to thrive. He has a purpose for you. You have a mission. If you keep your mission in mind, the right decisions will be obvious." I went on to share with him that we should all have long-term goals and vision. We should aim high because that's where the Lord wants us to be.

A lot of good opportunities will come your way, but you will not be able to take advantage of all of them, nor should you try. How do you know which opportunities are the best ones? Simply put, the ones which will enable you to further your mission. When we balance the opportunities and decisions, the energy required and the dividends earned, against our life's mission, then we can see our way clearly. The possibilities that look good, that might fit perfectly with another person's mission, suddenly are not what we need to pursue at this time. It's like I told my business friend: You must find a way to weigh daily decision against how it fulfills your life's calling. You must scrutinize the possible outcomes of your decisions in order to make sure that they provide wind in the sails of your dreams. If they do not, then they will likely blow you off course, eventually into dangerous waters and hidden riptides. You must know where you want to go before you can discover how to get there.

THE FAITH FACTOR

However, it's so much easier to go with the flow of the current, to get into that survive-the-day mindset. When the car breaks down and the kids need money for braces and you just argued with your spouse and your boss wants your report finished yesterday, that commitment to a greater vision and a higher mission may seem like a pie-in-the-sky dream. How do we take the steps needed to exceed the urgent demands that each day brings and instead heed the truly important calling set before us? All those who have truly succeeded will tell you it's faith, my friend, pure and simple. Faith is basically the conviction in a heart that refuses to plan to fail. Faith has one goal, and that is reaching what it hopes for. To accomplish that goal, faith will lead you into a plan. One of the greatest things I have learned about faith is that when you pray for a goal, God answers with a plan. He doesn't always give miracles as much as He gives a plan. He gave Joshua a plan to get through Jericho (Joshua 6:1–20). He gave Moses a plan to face Pharaoh (Exodus 3:7–10). He gave Elijah a plan when the brook dried up (1 Kings 17:2–16). He will give direction if we listen for it. Many people have failed to recognize the answer to prayer because they were looking for a miracle when God was waiting to answer with a plan.

It's like the old joke about the farmer whose land is flooded by a raging river. As the rising water swirls around him, he prays fervently for God to save him. Soon a man on a raft floats by and offers the farmer his hand. But the old farmer stays put and prays some more: Please, Lord, deliver me from this catastrophe. Climbing on top of his roof to escape the torrent, the farmer sees the sheriff waving to him from a small motor boat. Once again, he refuses to leave, confident that his faith in God will see him through. Finally, an Army helicopter flies overhead and lowers a rope ladder. The old man shakes his head, refusing to extend his hand and grasp the precious rung of survival. Instead, the farmer drowns and is taken to heaven, where he asks God, "I prayed so hard—I just knew you'd save me!" The Lord looks at him and says, "I sent you a raft, a motor boat, and a helicopter—what else do you want!"

Seriously, we must learn to realize that often the Lord's miracles do not descend in a puff of smoke with a drumroll. No, instead He fulfills his commitment by using His people to further His work. When we are good stewards who make the most of our talents, time, and treasure, our Father usually gives us an escape route from the flood waters that life brings.

"For I know the plans I have for you," declares the Lord, "plans to prosper you and not to harm you, plans to give you a hope and a future." (Jeremiah 29:11, NIV)

Without a plan, there is no target to aim for. We are shooting arrows into the woods haphazardly, content to empty our quiver without any return. Yet, the wise hunter does not waste arrows; he patiently observes, learns, and plans. Planners take careful aim and are rewarded by piercing the heart of their quarry. They strike the bullseye because they keep their eyes on the prize and plan diligently.

Perhaps the greatest example of planning comes from our Creator Himself. Although He created the original man and woman to enjoy intimacy with their Lord in the beautiful Eden He created for them, God nonetheless did not give up His desire to love us when Adam and Eve rebelled. He set in motion the gift of His Son, Jesus, in order to bridge the gap to heaven that was severed when the first humans disobeyed by devouring the forbidden fruit. This plan of redeeming His creation included prophecies foretelling the birth, life, and death of Jesus. It included all contingencies and was carried out perfectly by His Son.

Now you may be saying to yourself, "It's easy for God to develop and carry out His plan because He is perfect and sovereign! Well, I'm not!" That's where our faith comes in—the need to act on our plan, believing that we will succeed, maybe not like we expect but in the ultimate sense of our life's purpose.

SMART COUNSEL

Once He gives you a plan, you must have the courage to make the necessary decisions to conform your life into the image of the plan. I have learned that many people fail because they cannot make decisions. You cannot spend your life choosing; you must decide. The decisions you make must be informed. I see many leaders make the mistake of making decisions based on substandard information. Whoever or whatever is your source of information will affect the validity of your decision. A decision is no more sound than the data it is based upon. No one can make wise decisions with poor information. Surround yourself with people who will not waste your time with faulty information.

You absolutely must have wise and competent people around you. Please know that education, while invaluable, doesn't always indicate wisdom. Experience must accompany knowledge. Informed people with proven track records can assist you in channeling your efforts toward effective conclusions. Go where they are, listen to what they say, evaluate their opinions. Then make the final decision based on what's best for you.

This lesson was vividly illustrated for me recently as I was facing the final hours of my mother's life. I sat and listened to the doctors while they gave us many options about what they could do for and to my mother. They were very competent doctors whom I highly respected, but because I have pastored for many years and have been with many families in similar situations, I knew that the ultimate decision about what was best for our loved one could not be decided through medical information alone. You see, they knew medicine and operations, but my family and I knew my mother. The information was theirs to give, but the decision was ours to make. Always make your own decisions as you will be the one that has to live with the consequences of them.

It is important to gather information from several sources. By hearing many opinions but not immediately acting on any of them, you have time to separate fact from fodder. Believe me, you will always get a lot of fodder. Never go with the first information you get. Start soon enough in your decision-making process so that you can shop around. Remember, my friend, haste can cost you a great deal of embarrassment and cause a whole lot of mistakes.

> *Where no counsel is, people fall: but in the multitude of counselors there is safety.* (Proverbs 11:14, KJV)

Although you must have smart people around you who will tell you the facts, make sure they are not so aggressive that they make the final decision. The decision is yours. When you give that away, the game is over and your life is a pawn in the hands of others. As in my experience with my mother's medical team, the doctor gives you the test results and shares with you the options, but always know that while his advice should be heeded and respected, the decision is still yours. It is foolish to retain counsel and then not respect the counsel you retain, whether that counsel is an attorney, a doctor, or a marriage counselor. But hear me when I tell you that I can counsel the marriage, but you have to go home with your spouse. Whatever your desire may be, the decision is always yours.

Yes, no matter how good your counselors are, the ultimate decisions are still your own to make. This includes knowing when to wait, when to gather more data, and when to move and at what speed. When it comes to business and negotiations, always remember: Never take the first offer. Do enough research to discover what is the best and wisest choice. When you have done research and compared options, then you can make a decision. In order to maximize your right to choose, you must start early enough to enjoy the luxury and rewards of research. Most people who say they've been had have themselves to blame because they didn't do their homework. Ask questions, get opinions, and study the information. When all the facts are in, you can make a confident decision.

LEAVING THE COMFORT ZONE

You may be in full agreement that we must have smart counsel. You may ask yourself why anyone would deliberately surround themselves with ignorant or uninformed advisers. Usually, I believe it's not that we seek out bad counsel; it's simply that we settle for safe counsel. Often the best people with the most knowledge may challenge, stretch, and confront our previously held viewpoints. But that does not mean that they are to be avoided. On the contrary, that's why we need them! We must get over our fears of people who are smarter, more talented, or more experienced than we are and learn from them.

In order to make decisions that you will not regret, you must talk to competent people. What stops most people from approaching competent people is that they themselves feel ignorant when they are around them. But it is okay to be ignorant. What is not okay is to stay ignorant. I am constantly amazed by people who are intimidated by bright people. They surround themselves with people of lesser intelligence so that they appear superior. But what good is it to be the King of Fools?

The more you move into new arenas, the more you need a multitude of intelligent counsel. You need counselors who challenge you so that you can grow. You need to be around people you can learn from, people who push you to be more, even if it's uncomfortable at first. Don't run back to the familiar, mediocre interactions with people who do not challenge you to grow. Most people simply shoot too low in terms of whom they associate with, and they generally attain what they are aiming at. If you want the bullet to go higher, you must adjust the sights on your gun!

People with whom you are comfortable are generally those people

whom you relate to daily. That is fine if you are not going to build anything. But if you are going to build anything, if you are going to build
yourself financially, spiritually, and emotionally, you must go outside of
your comfort zone. If you do not, you will not have the information to
get beyond the familiar and attain the goal of your future. Only those
who are willing to be stretched beyond the ordinary toward the extra-
ordinary achieve their dreams.

MOVE IN THE MOMENT

We must have a plan and we must make decisions. We should surround
ourselves with wise counsel, gather the data, and be willing to stretch beyond our comfort zone. We need to prepare ourselves to make a move,
but eventually move we must. Indecisiveness is lethal to accomplishment. Yes, there is a time limit on how long you can consider which way
you want to go. You can't wait for things to happen to you; you must
make things happen for you.

I know you have seen some people succeed with no apparent effort;
however, what you have seen is luck. You cannot afford to build your life
plan on luck. You want to be blessed, but there is a difference between
being blessed and being lucky. Luck has nothing to do with what you
do—it is based totally on happenstance—whereas being blessed is a direct derivative of what you do to receive God's investment of favor. God
blesses what you do. He doesn't bless what you think or how you feel.
Remember that faith without works is dead by itself. In Psalm 1, David
teaches that the blessed man is a doing man. He is not lucky. He did
something that caused him to be blessed.

I certainly am not minimizing the place of prayer, as it is significant.
But might I suggest that prayer alone will never accomplish what work
is designed to do. Nor can work replace what prayer only can unleash.

Prayer releases the favor of God while work releases the force of man. When God's favor coincides with your force, you become unstoppable. I am always saddened by the many Christians who think that prayer replaces effort. It will not. It is not enough to pray for a better relationship with your daughter; you must also work at it. It is not enough to pray for restoration of your credit: you must also work at it. A total reliance on prayer, without the effort of work, is not biblical, nor is it practical. Your spirituality does not negate many practical truths; it will enhance them. Prayer can bypass the practical by accomplishing the supernatural, but more times than not, those of us who need to see fruit should be prepared to till the garden.

THE BIOLOGY OF STRATEGY

And he shall be like a tree planted by the rivers of water, that bringeth forth his fruit in his season; his leaf also shall not wither; and whatsoever he doeth shall prosper. (Psalm 1:3, KJV)

In Psalm 1:3 David compares us to a tree. Why a tree? A tree is stable and consistent. Regardless of the external changes, it remains steadfast. You must also be steadfast if you are going to receive the prosperity that comes from God. The tree is fed from underground resources. You also will see the feeding of your dreams with internal strategies and creativity, which are God's gifts to you. Your creativity will often be for your use alone. Those who try to imitate it will find that they cannot, for they don't have the passion, the vision, the innate drive within them. God gives you these gifts. He also gives you the strategy to effectively harness and utilize them. This strategy comes from your time with Him in prayer. God has a plan for you. God will tell you what you need to do to succeed. You just have to ask.

*If any of you lacks wisdom, let him ask of God, who gives to all liberally and with-
out reproach, and it will be given to him. (James 1:5, NKJV)*

The Lord provides glimpses of His plans for us when we seek Him.
But realize that not all of God's answers are in heaven. Some of them are
in you. You were created with creativity in your bones. The Lord de-
lights in using His children to fulfill His purposes. He has endowed you
with creativity so that you may use His gift to achieve greatness. The
answer you seek from Him may be lying within you, waiting for expression. Your frustration may often come from not challenging the gift He
has placed within you. Looking up is great, but once he has planted His
dreams in you, you would be wise to look within. The still small voice of
God, the still small voice of direction and creativity, is within the believing heart.

In Psalm 1, the tree's prosperity is largely a result of its ability to interact with others of its kind. Yes, you also will need to interact with
others of your kind. The act is called cross-pollination. This exchange is
not the stealing of others' ideas. As I explained, you can't have my fruit
or even my blossom, but there is something to be said for gaining a little of my pollen and using it to stimulate what God has in you.

All of us have had conversations or just been in the presence of someone whose pollen was so strong that we were strengthened through
that interaction. No matter how strong the tree is, if it is left alone with
no external resources to draw from, it will lose its full potential for fruit
bearing. It had the water, it had the sun, but it lacked the partnership to
produce. Are you in close proximity with growth partners? Are you involved with people who have fruit to draw from? Or are all your associates parasitic fruit pickers, drawing the life out of you and contributing
nothing to your dream? These hard questions must be asked because
they are the keys to maximizing all that God has available to you. In
order to be fruitful and prosper, you must be able to cross-pollinate with

others. When you are fruitful and associate with fruitful people, you enhance each other.

MASTER THE MISSION

As we have seen, if we want to maximize our moments, we must master our mission. We must strive for a clear vision of where God is calling us to and how to get there. Then we must lace up our shoes and start the journey, looking carefully for the landmarks of His leading along the path. We must learn from our mistakes, those dead ends and cul-de-sacs that entrap us, and get right back on the straight and narrow way that leads to our dreams. If we are truly to reach our full potential, we must not let others sway or deter us from our goals. Instead, we should draw off of the resources of others to give us smart counsel and good fruit. In return, we try to further them on their journeys as well.

If we will commit to mastering our mission, then so many of life's choices will come into focus clearer and sharper. It's like getting just the right prescription for your eyeglasses. The lenses take into account your own eyes' ability and then focus them accordingly. The result is a crisp image in clear focus, not the blurred edges of confusion. When we see where we're going and act in faith to get there with the Lord's help, then we enjoy the journey as much as the destination. We experience the rich freedom to reap the maximum that each day's moments bring to us.

I have chosen the way of truth; I have set my heart on your laws. I hold fast to your statutes, O Lord; do not let me be put to shame. I run in the path of your commands, for you have set my heart free. (Psalm 119:30–32, NIV)

SIX

DECIDE TO WIN

Considering our mission statement is a crucial first step in determining whether a relevant opportunity exists. Yet even after some decisions are eliminated as irrelevant or insignificant, many others remain. Indeed, within the many realms of our lives, we will be forced to make many necessary yet difficult choices. We cannot underestimate the vital importance of our life's decisions. You must realize that everything you are is the direct result of the decisions you have made or the decisions that were made for you. Like a stone skipped across the smooth, glassy surface of a beautiful, clear lake, each decision that we make initiates multiple ripples.

As we have seen, if we are to maximize our moments, we must take control of our life's decisions, because if we do not, someone else will. Not one of you reading this book wants to be someone else's pawn, someone else's puppet on a string. No, we must take charge of the major decisions of our lives and consider how we go about making final selections of the options at our disposal. Certainly, using our God-given common sense helps us survive these inevitable conflicts and dilemmas. When storm clouds gather in the late afternoon sky, it only makes sense to seek shelter and protect oneself. But as we know, not all situations are so obvious. Sometimes the sky turns gray, the thunder rumbles, but the rain never hits the ground. Sometimes we need more than common sense to guide us.

Obviously, we need a reliable compass to guide our paths. The factors we use in making life's decisions often determine whether the outcomes are more positive than negative. Although virtually everyone uses some kind of system to assist them in making their decisions, few have actually stopped to consider what has worked well and what has not. We live in an information age where more is supposedly always better, but the truth is that we must discern wisely, focusing only on the factors that allow us to fulfill our destinies. Too often, we have focused on too much information or have been distracted by the wrong kinds of information, or we have not investigated the credibility and authority of our sources. We have produced a generation that is bent on attaining knowledge, but they often lack the wisdom to regulate the knowledge that they attain.

So how can we consistently make the best decisions to maximize our potential? Although there is no perfect formula, there are some general guidelines that will enable you to make winning decisions. I call them the Ten Commandments for Winning Decisions because they are imperatives grounded in both biblical and practical wisdom. Just as the children of Israel needed the Ten Commandments in order to find their way back to God, through the desert to the Promised Land, so, too, do we need guidelines in making the most of our decisions. I humbly offer these ten principles based on my own experiences, my observations, and my interactions with a variety of different people, and my understanding of the Word of God. The more you use these principles to guide you, the less likely you are to wander aimlessly in the desert. Let's look at the list of all ten before I explain each one.

TEN COMMANDMENTS FOR WINNING DECISIONS

1. Control impulsiveness. Never make a permanent decision about a temporary situation.

2. Be aware of blind spots. Make sure that your emotions are not driving your decisions toward destruction.

3. Delegate with confidence. Surround yourself with people who are wise and competent. Empower them to perform and do not become intimidated by their expertise.

4. Consider all the options and accept responsibility for your final decision. Stop, look, and listen for wise counsel but always sift it through your own heart before final conclusions are made. Pray for guidance.

5. Never go to war where there are no spoils. Choose your battles wisely and make sure that what you fight for is worth the price you pay.

6. Be accurately informed. Make sure that you have all available facts before deciding anything. Conjecture will inevitably lead to crisis.

7. Contemplate the consequences. Consider all options and their possible results before acting on any of them.

8. Take calculated risks. Do not allow your expectations to exceed the practical potentials and realities of your resources. Hope for the best possible outcome or solution but be prepared for a loss.

9. Be cost-effective with time. If the return is not greater than the investment, then the endeavor is not worth your time.

10. Survive in order to thrive. Allow yourself a 10 percent ratio to be wrong, a 50 percent likelihood of betrayal, and a 100 percent commitment to survive it all.

THE HEAT OF THE MOMENT

1. Control impulsiveness. Never make a permanent decision about a temporary situation.

The first commandment reminds us that we must gain control over our impulsive reactions to other people, life events, and conflicts. Instead of merely wagging our tongues and mouthing off the first thing that pops into your head, you must use self-restraint and discernment. Rather than reacting to a situation, you must learn to respond to it. The difference is subtle but crucial. If your boss comes up to your desk and hands you a pink slip, your first reaction may be to slug him. However, after the immediate surge of anger has subsided, you realize that you have choices and that simply going with your rash inclination to punch his lights out may not be the best option. No, if you can keep your head above the water during the flood, then you realize the opportunities available even in difficult or painful circumstances. Perhaps you can negotiate some severance pay, a glowing letter of recommendation, or a referral to another company. Take the time to ask questions: Why are you being terminated, how could you have prevented it, what can you do different on the next job? Certainly you're entitled to feel angry at the situation, but avoid blaming yourself, your boss, and your company, and trust that there is a better opportunity opening just ahead of you. Exercise your faith as a bridge until the next door opens with its exciting offer. Be patient. Let the rain fall from that dark storm cloud, trusting that the water is necessary to nourish the seeds He has planted, which we can't even see yet.

I would have lost heart, unless I had believed that I would see the goodness of the Lord in the land of the living. Wait on the Lord; be of good courage, and He shall strengthen your heart; Wait, I say, on the Lord! (Psalm 27:13–14, NKJV)

It can be difficult to wait on the Lord. As most of us know, it is much easier in the heat of the moment to lose our calm, rational selves and turn into vengeful animals. Consequently, we make long-term decisions—either knowingly or unknowingly—about what is actually a temporary situation. Just because you lose one job, it does not mean you will remain unemployed for the rest of your life. Yet, if you slug your supervisor when he delivers the news, you may find it very difficult to find work for a while. You must not succumb to the convenience of impulsiveness, the tendency to choose immediate gratification. Instead, you must take a deep breath, remain quiet, and listen. Hear what is actually being said, not the script that may pop into your head for the occasion.

Instead of using our emotional reaction as license to feel sorry for ourselves and shift blame to others, we must learn to see beyond the eclipse of the present moment. Have you ever watched a solar or lunar eclipse? The way the shadow of the moon slides itself in front of the sun and blocks its wondrous light—it's simply amazing. The sun is still there, of course, but we cannot see it from our side. If this is the first solar eclipse you've ever seen, you might be afraid that the sun has been devoured and has disappeared forever. However, we learn that the moon passes in its orbit and the radiant flares of the great fireball returns. This, too, shall pass, as the old saying goes. We have to remember that the present catalyst, often a change or loss, shall also pass. Change is the only constant, and we must make peace with it if we are to succeed in our decision-making.

REARVIEW MIRRORS

2. Be aware of blind spots. Make sure that your emotions are not driving your decisions toward destruction.

In addition to impulsiveness, the second commandment reminds us that other emotional reactions can greatly hinder our ability to make effective decisions. Although we cannot totally divorce our emotions from the decisions we make, neither should we make them the North Star by which we guide our compass. Probably the most dangerous emotions that influence our decisions are anger, bitterness, and envy. Each one corrupts you into viewing circumstances as if they were images in fun-house mirrors. Each one creeps up alongside us like a car in the blind spot of our rearview vision. We must learn to use our rearview mirrors and turn our heads to look behind us before we make the decision to change lanes.

Anger robs us of our objectivity, usually at the very times we need to remain the most level-headed. When people do not follow through on their word, when they betray us with hypocritical actions, when they are well-intended but fail us nonetheless, it sets the blood to boiling and the mind to plotting vengeance. But we must realize that such anger can often blind us and keep us from making the best decision. Certainly we should allow ourselves to feel the anger, hurt, or frustration that comes swinging at us like a baseball bat, leaving deep bruises on the soul and psyche. As the apostle Paul reminds us in Ephesians, we should experience our anger but not succumb to temptation and give the devil a foothold (Ephesians 4:26–27). Allow your anger to pass through you like a current of electricity, but do not hold on to the current, because if you do, my friend, you are the one who will be shocked.

Refrain from anger and turn from wrath; do not fret—it leads only to evil. For evil men will be cut off, but those who hope in the Lord will inherit the land. (Psalm 37:8–9, NIV)

When we harbor anger, hurt, and disappointment, it usually festers into bitterness. I recall a woman I once knew—I'll call her Mrs. Parks—who ran her own catering business. As the number of members in our congregation began to swell rapidly, I asked if she might help out in the church kitchen during our fellowship suppers and potluck picnics. She refused and shook her head, her face flushed with color. When I asked why she couldn't help out in the kitchen, Mrs. Parks replied, "I can't be in the kitchen because Mrs. Smith is the church hostess, and she and I simply do not get along." My mind was puzzled, so I asked more questions. "But why, sister? What separates you and Mrs. Smith from getting along?" The woman began to hem and haw, but eventually she confessed that she was bitter toward Mrs. Smith because she had not asked Mrs. Parks to help out with the food preparation sooner! The woman prided herself on her good cooking and her ability to transform meals into special occasions, the very traits that had led to her successful catering company. Since Mrs. Smith had not recognized the woman's ability and immediately sought it for the kitchen committee, the woman felt hurt. She let her hurt fester like an embedded splinter until she identified Mrs. Smith as the root of all her ego's pain. Later, after I had talked to Mrs. Smith in private, I learned that she had simply assumed that Mrs. Parks was too busy running her catering business to help out. She would love to have the wonderful skills of Mrs. Parks! Eventually, the misunderstanding was worked out and both women became great friends. However, if some communication had not taken place, Mrs. Parks's decision to serve would have been blindsighted by her bitterness. The buried splinter of prideful disappointment would have festered into an infected wound of the soul.

> *Pursue peace with all men, and holiness, without which no one will see the Lord: looking diligently lest anyone fall short of the grace of God; lest any root of bitterness springing up cause trouble, and by this many become defiled. (Hebrews 12:14–15, NKJV)*

Finally, among the many emotions which can sneak up on us and edge us off the true path of our mission, lies the sticky trap of envy and covetousness. It's the comparison game which makes sure you always come up short. You compare yourself to others, thinking "if only." If only I had this car or that job, a different spouse, or more social status, then I would be successful. So in the meantime, you make decisions geared toward the wrong goal. It's not that you cannot be successful and have nice things, but if the basic motivation of your heart is to have what others have and to look like they do, then you will never learn to make the best decisions for your own heart's mission. Like the tar baby in the Uncle Remus classic fable, you will find yourself sticking more and more to goals that are not necessarily your own. Your goal will be attainment for its own sake, for the sake of keeping up with your neighbors, and showing off.

> *For where envy and self-seeking exist, confusion and every evil thing will be there.*
> *(James 3:16, NKJV)*

Do not allow your emotions to be the driving force behind your decisions. If you do, it will inevitably lead you off the chosen path of God's greatness toward the ditches of self-destruction.

SPOKES OF THE WHEEL

3. Delegate with confidence. Surround yourself with people who are wise and competent. Empower them to perform and do not become intimidated by their expertise.

Have you ever watched wheels turn? Most of us have joyfully watched as a small child plays with his toy truck on the living room floor. The small wheels on his truck turn and turn, covering inch after inch of the hardwood surface. Many of us have also sat outside and watched the traffic, the various cars and trucks rolling along our street. Their wheels turn, too, but the distance covered is not inches but miles. It's not surprising, of course, since their wheels' circumference is many times the size of the toy version.

I believe the circumference of our relational circles also determines how much ground we can cover. Imagine that you are a circle that can turn by itself. You roll along on your destination. But imagine if that circle suddenly becomes the hub of a much larger wheel. When spokes are attached, the wheel greatly expands its circumference and can cover much more ground. Similarly, we need to be surrounded with folks who are spokes to our wheel, enabling us to cover more ground.

Surrounding ourselves with a gifted network of responsible experts is not always easy. However, when we know that we have sought the best counsel possible, hired the most qualified employees, and commissioned competent professionals, then we are free to delegate with confidence. We do not have to worry about as many decisions as we would if we didn't have our network. We can empower them to make the decisions that they are best qualified to make, and we can trust their judgment because we have already discovered their trustworthiness.

It is like the metaphor that Paul uses in his epistle to the Romans: "For as we have many members in one body, but all the members do not have the same function, so we, being many, are one body in Christ, and individually members of one another. Having then gifts differing according to the grace that is given to us, let us use them" (Romans 12:4–6a, NKJV). Although our body parts are different—eyes, feet, earlobes, hands, knees—they are all necessarily interdependent. In order for a healthy body to function, each part does its job to the best of its ability. It does what it was created to do and relies on the other parts as they rely on it. Similarly, all believers are not alike, but all are necessary to form the body of Christ. We must each discover what we do best, pursue it, and share it with others. They in turn are pursuing their passionate calling and sharing their expertise with us. You are liberated to focus only on the decisions that you yourself are best qualified to make.

WHEN TO CROSS

4. Consider all the options and accept responsibility for your final decision. Stop, look, and listen for wise counsel but always sift it through your own heart before final conclusions are made.

When I was a kid growing up in West Virginia, my mother and father taught me to cross the street with great caution. Certainly, as a small tyke, I experienced the security that they were always with me when I crossed, our hands clasped firmly together. As an older boy, however, the day came when I could finally cross by myself. I'll never forget the important distinction my mother made for me that day. She said, "Anyone on two legs can cross the street, but only one who looks before he leaps knows *when* to cross. You must stop, look, and listen before you step off the curb."

The parallels are obvious but nonetheless profound for how you make your decisions. In our country today, anyone can decide to start a business. But only a wise man or woman knows when the time is right to start their kind of business. They talk to people, do research, and study the market and the competition's products. And then when the right moment comes along, they seize it and take the plunge for themselves. If the business should fail, they accept the full responsibility because they did everything that they could in order to make it succeed.

These days it's almost as if some folks want to make decisions without knowing all the options so that if they fail, they have an excuse. But these kinds of people will never know their full potential because they're unwilling to take the risk to be true to themselves. If we must have someone else to blame because we are so insecure in ourselves, then we will always settle for mediocre lives. Winning decisions are the result of the careful analysis of all possible viewpoints and the initiative to act on your selection. Keep in mind that lots of people can give you advice or tell you their experiences, but only you can make the decision. Don't fool yourself into thinking that you have no choices or that you must do what so-and-so says because she's the expert. We always have choices. Even during difficult circumstances and painful trials, we still have choices about how we respond. We are never bound to another's suggestion, no matter who they are. We must allow ourselves the time needed to stop and pause for reflection, to look at all possibilities, to listen to our network of advisers, and then to step off the curb with boldness. Sift all the options through your own heart in order to know what is right for you. And never forget to pray, as God is always available for comfort and guidance. Start with prayer, and you'll end up okay.

> *If any of you lacks wisdom, let him ask of God, who gives to all liberally and without reproach, and it will be given to him. (James 1:5, NKJV)*

PRIZE FIGHTS

5. Never go to war where there are no spoils. Choose your battles wisely and make sure that what you fight for is worth the price you pay.

Have you ever met someone who seemed to thrive on conflict? They are always picking on others, arguing, disagreeing, trying to get something started. They fight just for the sport of it, not because they passionately believe in a particular cause or want the gold trophy. These folks usually make poor decisions and others learn to ignore them and not take them seriously. We learn that they are really in a battle with themselves, with their need to always win in order to feel good about themselves. But as we've seen, self-confidence does not come from merely putting everyone else flat on the mat just to show how strong you are. Self-confidence, including confidence in our ability to make good decisions, comes from within, from wisdom, faith, and awareness. Fighting a battle without anything at stake is a mute point, as futile as chasing the wind or trying to pour salt on a bird's tail feathers.

No, part of the art of making winning decisions is knowing when to fight and what you're fighting for. I recall a situation with one of my children's teachers in elementary school. When my son came home with a long face, I asked him what was wrong. He revealed that he felt his teacher had been too hard on him that day. She had forced him to read in front of his class even though he was embarrassed and shy. I immediately reacted like any father would: the proud papa who wants to defend his little cub. My son encouraged me to talk to his teacher and tell her to leave him alone. He wanted me to tell her that he shouldn't have to read in front of everyone if he didn't want to. I told him that I would like to wait another day or two and then talk to his teacher. During that interval, I considered what was at stake. I could take on his teacher and defend my little angel, which was how I had reacted inside. But I asked myself, What would I gain by doing this? It not only seemed that I might not have anything to win in this battle, I clearly might lose the respect of his teacher. On the other hand, if I cooled off a day or two and then talked to her calmly, maybe I could understand the motive in her handling of my son. Maybe this battle was not a battle at all. As I came to find out from his teacher later, all the children were required to read in front of the class—my son just happened to go first. As she listed the benefits of practicing oral literacy, I more than agreed with her approach. We even worked together so that my son could practice reading aloud more at home, a decision he didn't like at first but one that was ultimately for his good.

Fighting a battle without spoils is like trying to douse water on an empty, dilapidated, condemned old shack that's burning to the ground. Assuming no one is in any danger from its flames, we are better off without the old eyesore. There's nothing there worth saving. Instead, we should save our strength and energy for the time when it's our home burning or when someone is trapped inside.

> *Do you not know that those who run in a race all run, but one receives the prize? Run in such a way that you may obtain it. (1 Corinthians 9:24, NKJV)*

Too often, I've seen too many people fighting the wrong battles at the wrong time. They waste their time and expend their energy fighting other people's battles for them. They themselves held no stake in the outcome, but they felt compelled to jump in anyway. Or else they fight their own battle but don't realize that they've lost the war until it's too late. Although most generals don't talk about it, they all assess what they consider to be an "acceptable loss" for any given battle. If the number of lives lost in order to win a particular battle is too costly, they realize that it may ultimately prove self-defeating—they could then lose the war even though the last skirmish was a success.

We must use discernment and stay focused on our goals. Only then can we make deliberate choices about whether or not a fray is worthy of our attention. If we keep our eyes on the prize that God sets before us, then we will realize that some things simply aren't worth our time. They are only there to distract us. Becoming a "prize fighter" will lead you to make better, wiser decisions.

TRIPLE A

6. Be accurately informed. Make sure that you have all available facts before deciding anything. Conjecture will inevitably lead to crisis.

I've stressed the importance of relying on wise, trustworthy counsel, and the necessity of controlling impulsiveness. Nevertheless, even with these principles in mind, many people will continue to jump to conclusions too soon and make significant choices merely on conjecture. Sometimes overeager, sometimes impatient, sometimes afraid to wait any longer, these folks often jump the gun and make choices limited by their present perspective rather than the larger picture, which would emerge if they only sought more data and waited patiently. Patience is perhaps one of the most difficult skills to practice when it comes to decision-making.

> *I waited patiently for the Lord; and He inclined to me, and heard my cry. (Psalm 40:1, NKJV)*

How can we cultivate patience when forced to make tough choices? When the pressure has built to an unbearable level, how can we remain calm and collected? I believe there are three important steps in gaining a patient perspective. First, we must *ask* the right questions. Next we must *answer* those questions based on the counsel of the other spokes on our wheel. Finally, we must *act* when the time is right and we know we are acting on both the best and most comprehensive information available. The Triple A's: ask, answer, act.

Knowing the right questions to ask is an art in itself. Too often, you remain silent and keep your questions to yourself because you're afraid of embarrassing yourself by asking a "dumb question." You're afraid others will laugh at your ignorance or at your naivete. Well, I learned the hard way something one of my teachers once told me. After I had scored lower than I'd hoped on my final exam, I asked the teacher for the correct answers to the questions I had missed. He told me and then asked, "Why didn't you ask in class if you didn't understand this concept here?" I just hung my head. He seemed to understand my shame and compassionately continued, "There are no stupid questions. If you want to know something, that's valid reason enough to ask it courageously. Chances are good that someone else has the same questions and the same reluctance to ask because of their fears of what others will think. The only stupid questions are the ones that go unasked because we're either too afraid or too ignorant to know what to ask. Always, always, ask." Those words have stuck with me, and I encourage you to own them as your own. Be curious, inquisitive, and hungry for all the pieces of the puzzle before you start deciding where to begin.

Ask and it will be given to you; seek and you will find; knock and the door will be opened to you. Everyone who asks receives; he who seeks finds; and to him who knocks, the door will be opened. (Matthew 7:7–8, NIV)

Finding the answers to your questions may be even harder than knowing what to ask. You have to sift through the chaff of others' misinformation (once again, highlighting the necessity of having reliable counsel), the surface impression of the data, and the possible relationships among the pieces of information in order to make a winning decision. Forge ahead, though, and you will soon see a clearer picture emerging, the true image that coincides with your calling and your participation in this particular choice.

Finally, once you have asked and answered as many questions as possible, it is time to act. Once you're confident that you have the most information available, and that it is reliable, do not linger in the shadows of fear, waiting for a spotlight from heaven to provide you with insurance. No, it is then time to act, my friend. If the endeavor fails, you can relax in the knowledge that you did everything possible to make a wise decision. You must then view the failure as an opportunity to learn something needed for the next stage of the game. On the other hand, if the endeavor succeeds, you must remember the important steps you took to make it happen so that you can repeat the process the next time.

WHAT IF

7. Contemplate the consequences. Consider all options and their possible results before acting on any of them.

Now, it may seem like I'm talking out of both sides of my mouth as I shift from commandment six to commandment seven. I just told you not to base decisions on conjecture and second-guessing, and that is so true. However, I think it's absolutely vital that we engage our imaginations in the process of making winning decisions. We must learn to imagine the possible outcomes of various options that we have at our disposal for any given decision. What kind of chain reaction might occur if we make this decision? How will it either fulfill or distract us from our mission control? What will the effects of this decision be a year from now? Five years from now? At the end of our lives? For especially life-altering decisions, I like to employ what I call the rocking-chair test. I imagine that I'm an old, old man at the end of my life sitting on my front porch in my rocking chair, remembering the good and the bad times of my youthful endeavors. How will I remember this present decision? What kind of man will it have shaped me into at the twilight of my life? How will my relationship with God be affected, with my family, friends, and co-workers?

A friend who is a novelist tells me about another game he plays that helps him to make decisions. He explains that his favorite game to play as he gets started on a new storyline is "What if?" "What if this character did this and that character responded by being upset and then quitting her job?" He goes on and on down the possible flow charts of causality, trying to discover the story that best fits his characters, his themes, and his interest. He simply claims to investigate the possibilities until he stumbles upon the way he believes it must have happened to the characters. My writer friend tells me that he plays the same game when he is forced to make decisions. "What if I take this option? Or what if I make this decision instead? What will my own life's story look like as a result?" he asks himself. My friend insists, and I agree, that we must exercise our imaginations, not just our intellects, in the decision-making process.

> *Keep sound wisdom and discretion, so they will be life to your soul and grace to your neck. Then you will walk safely in your way, and your foot will not stumble.* (Proverbs 3:21b–23, NKJV)

Thinking through the potential consequences of our decisions often prevents more problems from occurring down the road. If we can see clearly the possible outcomes, then we can make better long-term choices than if we are only focused on the near-sighted present.

RISKY BUSINESS

8. Take calculated risks. Do not allow your expectations to exceed the practical potentials and realities of your resources. Hope for the best possible outcome or solution but be prepared for a loss.

I knew a man who liked to wager on his poker-playing ability with his buddies. He certainly enjoyed the fellowship, but he also seemed to win consistently. Without endorsing his sport, I asked him the secret of his success. He said, "I keep a little fund that's all my own just for my poker games. I make sure I pay the bills, take care of my family's needs first, and then I can assess how much I can afford to lose. I never bet more than I'm prepared to lose." It struck me then that his method applies to most of our decision-making. Even though we try to imagine the outcomes of our choices, we can never know exactly what the Lord will bring to pass until He allows it. So in many ways we must think through the potential negative consequences of our best-case decisions and prepare for resultant losses. It's basically a budget for gambling: You must be willing to take risks, but you cannot risk everything every time. You have to develop a sense of timing and saving so that when a good opportunity presents itself, you can take that calculated risk.

This principle reminds me of the parable of the talents that Jesus tells (Matthew 25:14–30). The master of the house is leaving for a long trip to a foreign country. He delegates the responsibility of managing his goods to three different servants. To the first he gives five talents, to the second he gives two talents, and to the third servant he gives one talent. When the master returns, he brings the three servants before him to account for his treasure. The first servant proudly hands him back ten talents instead of five; he doubled the master's money and the master is pleased. The second, likewise, produces four talents from the original two. The master is very pleased with them both. But the third servant cowers and says, "I was afraid, and went and hid your talent in the ground. Look, there you have what is yours" (Matthew 25:25). That master is furious! The third servant took no risks whatsoever and yielded no return on what his master had entrusted to him.

I believe we should not be reckless or careless with the resources that are attached to the decisions we make. But neither should we bury them in the ground because we become paralyzed by fear, overwhelmed at the possible options and consequences. If we have done our homework and have confidence in our mission, our advisors, and ourselves, then we can risk with confidence as well.

TAKE STOCK OF THE CLOCK

9. Be cost-effective with time. If the return is not greater than the investment, then the endeavor is not worth your time.

The most precious commodity that anyone of us possesses is our time. We do not know how long our days will be, so we must have our feet on the ground of the present while having our backs warmed by the rays of the past and our eyes focused on the vision of the future. When we're young, we often do not realize the true value of each hour in every day. We squander time, wandering here and there, feeling like we have all the time in the world to discover what the future holds. However, as we mature, we come to recognize that no matter how rich or poor we are, time on this earth is more valuable than gold.

When decisions come our way, we must assess the cost of both making various choices as well as living with their consequences in the only truly universal currency: time. If we are going to have to spend so much time becoming educated enough to see all the options, and we see that the outcome is minimal, then perhaps we should delegate the decision to someone else. Or perhaps it is a decision that will take care of itself in due time.

Too often, I'm afraid we spin our wheels like hamsters on a treadmill, expending a lot of energy as the hours tick by but getting no further along in our journeys. It's like the thrifty shopper I knew, a friend of our family, who prided herself on her ability to clip coupons and save hundreds of dollars on her family's necessities. However, the woman was never home—she was never there for her family because she was always driving to a dozen different stores on opposite sides of town to use her precious coupons and save a few pennies. This woman later realized that the enormous amount of time she spent, not to mention the gasoline and energy, was not worth the quarter off a loaf of bread. People like my friend who waste gas, time, and energy by driving to all the different stores to use their coupons lose more than they save. No, we must think like an accountant, assessing the minutes, hours, days, weeks, and months on our calendar. How we spend our time should become increasingly cost-effective the older and, hopefully, more mature we get. We realize the short breath of time we are given and use it to its maximum potential.

> *As for man, his days are like grass; as a flower of the field, so he flourishes. For the wind passes over it, and it is gone, and its place remembers it no more. (Psalm 103:15–16, NKJV)*

SURVIVAL OF THE FITTEST

10. Survive in order to thrive. Allow yourself a 10 percent ratio to be wrong, a 50 percent likelihood of betrayal, and a 100 percent commitment to survive it all.

In order to make winning decisions, we must persevere. We must assess our habits from the past and determine to change and mold them according to our mission statement for the future. If we stay mired in the muddy pit of self-defeat, guilt, and shame over past missed opportunities and wrong choices, then we will never experience the freedom to restore our trajectory to our destiny's flight plan. You will never soar when you're too busy wallowing in self-pity and blame-shifting.

In order to survive and thrive, you must allow yourself to fail and allow a margin of error. As we have seen with the other nine commandments, we try to minimize our potential for failure as much as we possibly can, but we must still be prepared for defeat. Allowing a ten percent margin for failure allows us to balance informed optimism with cautious realism. It also keeps us humble and reminds us from whence we came. There's nothing worse than a successful person who becomes haughty and forgets that God is the one who blesses our endeavors. We make our plans, but the Lord decides ultimately whether we will succeed or fail according to His purposes, not ours. In Proverbs we are reminded, "Do not boast about tomorrow, for you do not know what a day may bring forth" (27:1, NKJV). No matter how well we plan or how effective our decisions, we must always leave room for the Lord to work.

The next margin that we must keep in mind in order to survive and thrive is the margin of betrayal. Not only must we leave room for our unexpected disappointments and unknown variables, we must also realize that we will inevitably be hurt deeply by other people. Perhaps they deceived us into believing they were trustworthy, perhaps they began sincerely and became corrupted by jealousy or greed—in either case, you will feel the scorpion's sting of poisonous betrayal as you wade along the shores of life. It's usually the people we love most or trust implicitly who have the greatest power to betray us. We must deal with the hurt, anger, and disappointment without allowing them to blindfold us to the long-range consequences. A 50 percent margin for betrayal may seem too high to you, but trust me, my friend: If you live long enough, you will discover how fickle and selfish the human heart can be. Do not be deterred from your life's goals when this happens. Like a child who has learned to walk and gets tripped by a bully, we must get right back on our feet and continue on our journey. We will be a little sore, a bit bruised at first, but the scabs heal and we are stronger for having survived the fall.

Now brother will betray brother to death, and a father his child; and children will rise up against parents and cause them to be put to death. And you will be hated

by all men for My name's sake. But he who endures to the end shall be saved.
(Mark 13:12–13, NKJV)

Finally, you must pledge to yourself that no matter what circumstances transpire, or which decisions flop miserably, you will survive. You will rise up and learn from the circumstance, draw close to your God, and if nothing else, thank Him for the breath pumping through your lungs, for the blood coursing through your veins. Thank Him that the present season of disaster has not lasted forever and will not last forever into the future. Thank Him for the blessings you do have, for if you think about it, you will realize you have many.

When I realize the long list of gifts that remain in my life even in the midst of my trials, defeats, and disappointments, then I become lighter, more able to see the big picture and not just the immediate thumb's hangnail in front of my eyes. Gratitude is a sure antidote to self-pity and defeatism. An attitude of thanksgiving will always elevate you back to a position of viewing your life's decisions more clearly. Thank God for what you have accomplished so far and what you will accomplish again.

> *My brethren, count it all joy when you fall into various trials, knowing that the testing of your faith produces patience. But let patience have its perfect work, that you may be perfect and complete, lacking nothing. (James 1:2–4, NKJV)*

All of us on life's journey will inevitably face failure, betrayal, and the temptation to give up our dreams and settle for a dreary existence of compromise. But we must call on the Lord, thank Him for our many blessings, and embrace His peace, which truly surpasses anything we can explain. Then we get up the next morning and continue on our journey, a little sore, a little stiff, but nonetheless ready to walk each step required for that day.

THE OBEDIENT INGREDIENT

If you keep these laws impeccably, there will be a few rabbits that still get under the fence. When they do sneak in and nibble at your garden, assess the damage, and go on. Remain faithful and obedient to the calling that you have answered by picking up this book in the first place. Remember the true mission of your heart. Strive for your dreams despite the setbacks. Continue to obey these principles and others that God reveals to you. The one ingredient that you can control beyond a shadow of a doubt is to remain obedient.

Whatever you do, please do not indulge yourself in the expensive art of depression nor the drunken stupor of denial. Avoid the wasted days of self-flagellation. You would be amazed what can be done with the leftover moments of a bad experience. If they are captured quickly, you can redeem many mistakes with quick thinking and definitive efforts rather than pity parties that come complete with sad songs, sorrowful hats, and sour cakes.

Stand up to the music, face the band, and decide what you have left after the mistakes you have made. Make the best decision you can with the choices you have left, and keep living. Chances are the setback is just a setup for a greater opportunity for which you will need the precious experience you have just gained. If we embrace these opportunities as learning experiences, it will often enrich your life so dramatically that you need not go through this same painful experience again.

My friend, I cannot guarantee that you will always succeed by following these Ten Commandments. But I do believe that if you follow them consistently, they will help you unleash your full potential and maximize the most of each and every opportunity in the days ahead.

SEVEN

WINGS LIKE
EAGLES

Wherefore seeing we also are compassed about with so great a cloud of witnesses, let us lay aside every weight, and the sin which doth so easily beset us, and let us run with patience the race that is set before us, looking unto Jesus the author and finisher of our faith. (Hebrews 12:1–2, KJV)

Reread the verse from the twelfth chapter of Hebrews. Our life is the race set before us, and it is a serious race indeed, so how can we possibly *run with patience!* How do we harness the kinetic energy of the soul in a calm, steadfast way? How can you be patient when you know that this is *your* moment? Let's explore the challenge of the author of Hebrews to relax in the midst of the stress brought about by demanding times.

It is interesting to note that this challenge in the twelfth chapter of Hebrews comes after the most powerful definitions of faith in the Bible. It is no accident that at the end of a powerful dissertation about faith, the writer now starts the next chapter by telling us to relax while we run. It is simply a matter of faith that makes it possible for the faithful to relax in the midst of the stressful situations of life. Faith is essential to create the ability to channel your strength rather than frantically hurl it at problems and challenges. Power without control is energy that is not harnessed. Its strength is impressive, but its results are not productive. If any man is going to be productive, his strength has to be harnessed, his vision has to be focused, and his stride has to be steady. A steady stride connotes a patient, relentless progression toward a goal. A wild, car-weaving, horn-blowing person may pass you on the road, but have you ever noticed that sooner or later, down by the corner or up at the traffic light, you catch up to him? Though your speed was less, your gait was steady. You see, my friend, the race is not given to the swift. It is that steady, relentless stride that takes home the prize.

I returned and saw under the sun that the race is not to the swift, nor the battle to the strong, nor bread to the wise, nor riches to men of understanding, nor favor to men of skill; but time and chance happen to them all. (Ecclesiastes 9:11, NKJV)

SOUL STRETCHES

As stretching is essential to muscle so that it can conquer the demands of the race, so, too, does the soul need to be stretched to successfully meet the demands of life. God allows us to have a series of stretching experiences that prepare us for the race. Like the runner leaning against the wall to give his muscles resistance training, we have all had to push against immovable forces. Every so often, your soul will hit a wall. No amount of strength, no amount of pressing, will move the problem. This is a soul stretch.

Have you been stretched yet? I bet you have. The things that come into your life and pull you are not always the real test. They often are the warm-ups that prepare you for future challenges. They are your point of reference that keeps you from panic when you are in the midst of the real race. God never allows a person to run for Him or with Him who hasn't been stretched in his thinking, stretched in his faith, and stretched in his ability to live and love. When you face a problem that will not move, always remember to take a deep breath and let the air out real slow. Remember that God is stretching your soul.

Soul stretches are prerequisites for winning the race. It is the stretching of the soul that enables us to face situations that we think will kill us but don't, endure times when we think we won't make it but do. We all will face difficult times, but they are just the deep knee bends of life. They stretch and challenge the soul and enable us to get loose enough to perform successfully.

DOMINOES OF DESPAIR

Although we can know this truth—that God stretches our souls during trials—it is still not easy to face difficult situations. When hard times come for us, as they inevitably will, it feels so much easier to succumb to what I call the "dominoes of despair." Have you ever seen those massive domino chains that some people set up? With one plink of the finger, each domino topples over until the entire chain of once-erect blocks is leveled. Trying times can burn our lives into the domino effect. We become *disappointed* with some event or relationship in our lives. As the trial lingers and we feel the burn of our soul's muscles, we topple into *discouragement* and release our expectations for things to change. Finally, as we feel the impossibility of moving the object against which we lean, we may succumb to *despair,* the final domino in the chain. We feel powerless and hopeless and don't know how to see our way clear. Instead of running a race, it feels like we are swimming under the surface of an ocean of Jell-O.

I know this firsthand, my friend. Let me share with you some details of the most harrowing valley I have experienced. I had just come in from

a speaking engagement at Howard University. I had been there to motivate a group of young college students. I was asked to challenge them to
persevere by relying on their rich heritage and strong faith in God to
climb the stretching academic Alps to the pinnacle of optimum potential and possibility. They had given me a gracious reception, and I felt as
if I had accomplished with some dexterity what I had been commissioned to do. I had bonded with the audience, interacted with the president of the university, met many of the faculty, and was back in my
hotel room attempting to relax from the resultant stress and fatigue of
too many hours of travel and not enough rest. I climbed into the bed that
night like a bear preparing to hibernate for the winter. I do not know
when I drifted off, but finally I had slipped into the catatonic state of
sleep that my weary soul had long awaited. At last, my frame had
meshed with the mattress, my head had become one with the pillow,
and I was gone.

Suddenly, as I fell deeper into sleep, in a dream I saw my mother
lying in a bed that was all covered in white. It was not a natural white but
that heavenly, fluorescent white that reminded me of death or the here-
after. I was sitting by her bed, and she was lying strangely on her back.
She wasn't dead, but she was very still, listening intently to my conversation as I began to speak. In the midst of my monologue, she turned toward me in a movement that reminded me of someone who has had a
stroke. She spoke to me a motherly assurance that God wasn't nearly
through blessing me. And with that, she returned back to her original
position, and I woke up with a start.

I knew instantly she was in trouble. My heart was racing. It was about
two in the morning, and I knew that I would have no more sleep that
night. As I fought to control the wave of fear that engulfed my heart, I
thought to myself, "She moved like she had had a stroke!" I reached for
the phone; my heart was in my throat. It wasn't a normal dream. I called
her and woke her out of a sound sleep. My mother is probably one of the

few people in the world whom I could infringe upon by calling in the middle of the night and who would not find the call intrusive. As usual, she was glad to hear from me and awoke immediately. I talked to her until daylight, finally sharing with her my concerns for her health and some small details about the dream that had alarmed me. She assured me she was fine, but I was still troubled as I flew home that next morning.

Three days later, while I was preaching, I looked at her face and noticed that her jaw was twisted into a grimace. I almost lost track of my message as I feared that she was in trouble. She fell asleep during the service that day; it was the kind of hard sleep of someone in a comalike state. My wife confirmed my concern after the service. I had a nurse check her immediately. The strokelike symptoms were so apparent that even the nurse was almost positive that it was a stroke. Needless to say, I wanted her tested to be sure of what had happened and assess the degree of the damage.

I was at home when the call came. It was not a stroke as I had feared. Before I could sigh in relief, the doctor said it was worse than that. She said, "I am afraid your mother has a brain tumor." I will never forget the nauseating feeling that rose up in me. It seemed as if all the air had been sucked out of the room. In my life's journey, suddenly my brisk, confident stride was halted by a brick wall. The floor started spinning and the ceiling began to swirl. I do not remember what else was said because at that moment nothing else mattered except the fact that my mother had a brain tumor. I was so sick that I ran out into the night air trying to breathe.

So the drama began, with us on a rollercoaster ride from Hell itself. A few days later, I watched the doctors roll my mother into surgery as I sat outside with my other siblings and tried not to think of them sawing through the skull of the woman who taught me to read and write. Knowing that she had one of the best neurological teams available in the country brought me little comfort. My stomach had turned to oatmeal, and it had begun to bubble and scorch deep down inside the lining of my bowels.

Before the operation, my mother had requested that I go in the operating room with her. The doctors, of course, refused. When I asked her why, she said, "I think that I might slip away. I want you to be close enough to call my name if I were dying. I know that if you were in the room and I heard your voice, if there were any way in the world I could come back, I know I would come back to you." She said, "I love you so much that if I didn't come back to you, it would mean I couldn't come back at all." Her words burned through me like hot wax on tender skin. My heart exploded like a dam bursting as I fought back the tears that threatened to flood my face. It was in that instance that I confirmed that there is no love like a mother's love. It is not clouded by romance, or dependent like a child's. Life has no transaction that enriches one's development like the ringing sound of a mother's loving affirmation. As I waited while she was in surgery, her words replayed in my mind. I realized that I would never taste a sweeter love. I suddenly recognized after forty years of living that she had loved me madly all of my life. I was sick with worry and dizzy with fear. How could I lose her? How would I face a day not knowing that she was there? My wife had just lost her mother. It had taken a terrible toll and now death had come to knock again. I would like to say that my faith was so invincible and impeccable that I was calm and detached, but that would not be even remotely true. The reality was I was just absolutely sick.

Nine hours later, my mother emerged out of the surgery. They rolled her into the recovery room and soon a weak smile eased across her face, and with trembling little hands she gripped mine and tried to see through the eye that had nearly seen the Lord Himself a few hours before. She was frail but, oh, so strong. She had resisted death like she was playing a chess game with an old master. I recalled that she had told the doctor when she went in, "If you do your job, I will do mine." He had and she had, and most of all God had done a marvelous job of sustaining her. He was the secret weapon that defeated the terrible foe. It seemed as if it was destined to be happy ending. We celebrated feverishly; we thought it was all behind us. And it almost was.

VALLEY OF THE SHADOW

Just as she was recovering from the surgery and we were recovering from the drain put on our hearts and souls, the turbulence of trials jolted us out of our comfortable seats. The next domino toppled us into discouragement, for then came the complications. The spinal chambers in the brain began to back up, the bleeding started, and the next surgery came. Doctors put a shunt in her skull that ran down to her abdomen. It later collapsed and they put in another, and then another. Each time my mother arose, but she was a little weaker. The multiple surgeries caused swelling on the brain each time.

The hospital stay turned into a prolonged, extended, tedious journey into the tragic, depressing rhythm of affliction that causes a family to drag into the hospital almost mechanically. It became the kind of stay that lasts long enough for the family to learn the shifts, personality, and preferences of each nurse and attendant. We would take her home, only to have to bring her back when more complications arose. We took her home, we brought her back. Around and around we went, over and over again. The process continued for months.

My mother had made me promise that no matter what happened I would continue to preach. She didn't want to be the cause of a digression from my calling. I made that promise, but it was a hard one to keep. I continued to preach, teach, lecture, write lyrics, books and magazines, organize a play, and run back and forth to the hospital. I still shudder when I see tapes from those times when I was preaching outwardly and secretly at my wits' end inwardly. It wasn't a matter of falling apart on the outside. No, I was better trained than that. But even when you are going on outwardly, there can exist a deterioration of the soul that no one sees but God alone.

She was so weak I thought she would die in my arms. I can still feel her head on my chest as she stood resting her head on me trying to get her balance, leaning on me like a child in trouble. Her body was as limp as a dishrag. Her eating had almost stopped. She had lost all control of her body's functions. The adult diapers, the baby food, the accidents on my carpet, my floor, and often down my leg—sad markers of a steady decline. Nurses and doctors had poked her everywhere she could be poked or prodded. She was not getting better, and we knew it. It stripped our heart of its song and crippled our ability to remember better days or any days for that matter. We struggled to remember what day it was; in the hospital they all seemed to be the same. Mother struggled to re-member which one of us was feeding her. That original dream of mine was unfolding like a nightmare in my life. No wonder I had awakened in such a panic. This was a soul stretch that tested every muscle and fiber of my inner being. I had never walked through such a deep valley of the shadow of death before.

I was amazed that I had lived all these years and had not realized how degrading sickness is for those we love. I tried to make light of it for Mom. I didn't want her to be embarrassed, but it really didn't matter. She wasn't embarrassed because she was too sick to know that she had soiled my suit and I had to change for church. I sat in the car in front of the church and cried. My mother was dying, her body was weak, her blad-der was gone, her stool was water, and I had to go in those doors and smile at the people and preach. It wasn't fair. But, then, is life fair? I didn't realize that life is so fair that into each life the rain of persecution falls without discretion. I preached with fervor and vigor. No one knew that while I preached I could still feel her trembling head laying on my chest fighting for strength and balance, and I didn't tell them.

My brother, my sister, and I took turns working through family crises. My wife and children all labored to hold all the ends together while I continued to teach, work, write, encourage others. Every now and then, when no one was around, I sat on the floor and washed my face in tears. My soul was being stretched beyond what I felt it could bear, and it was aching like an overextended muscle. My heart was cracked, and inside I thought I was being pulled apart. I was the television minister of millions, the pastor of thousands, the father of five, the Chief Executive Officer of three companies, and the husband of one. That was a lot to maintain at the same time, and I had to hide my pain.

The dominoes continued to fall and our souls teetered on the brink of despair. I recall an especially soul-wrenching moment. I had just moved my mother in with us. She was upstairs and she called out to me in fear and agony. She could not see; she didn't know where she was. She was afraid. I climbed into her bed like I had done when I was a child having a bad dream. But this time it was no dream for either of us. I held her in my arms until her fears subsided and she fell asleep. I dragged myself out of the bed and went to my room, tired and empty and alone. My soul screamed, but my lips were pursed and not a sound escaped into the night. Tribulation was working on me, stretching me, and I couldn't dare scream out, could I?

I thought it would get better, but it didn't. In fact, three hospitals, eight doctors, three ambulance rides, one medical flight, and a twenty-one-day stint in one of Charlotte's best hospitals could not put my mother back together again. I thought I would die, but I didn't. I thought I would come unglued, but I couldn't. I thought I would lose my mind and faint, but I just stood there instead, watching her wilt away. She started trembling more and more like she had Parkinson's disease. She didn't complain nor did I; we just walked through it.

HOPE WITHIN HEARTACHE

Finally, I got the strength to accept the things I could not change. The Scriptures came alive in my pain. They thrived in my trauma. I found out that when pain doesn't go away, your endurance increases. I learned that when things are really bad, you tolerate things that are mind-boggling. For the first time, I knew what to do when pain won't stop. I finally realized that every story doesn't have a happy ending, at least not the one we want at the time. Nonetheless, I began to see how to stop the domino effect of my despair. Hope glimmered through in God's Word, in the help from friends and members of my congregation. Rest for my runner's fatigue was still a long way off, but I could at least keep focusing on the next step in front of me.

Then, like a tug-of-war between hope and despair, another jerk from the darkness. The doctor said that all of those surgeries, the swelling of her brain, and the invasive treatments had expedited Mom's aging process. They diagnosed her as having developed Alzheimer's, as if the tumors and the shunts were not enough. The word scared me. It sounded so terrible. No one talks about it. Those who have loved ones who have it say little because people do not want to know, and they sure don't come to visit.

I never knew that her life would have this huge detour toward the end of her journey. The part of her brain that commands the swallow-ing function wasn't operating, so she sat for hours with food in her mouth, which she would neither relinquish nor swallow. My brother, my sister, and I watched as the woman who had given her life to edu-cating others lay struggling to differentiate one of us from the other, a lemon from an orange, one year from another, and on and on and on.

Well, I wasn't going to tolerate it. My desperation blistered into anger.

Here I was the Chief Executive Officer for several companies that I founded myself. After all, I am the Senior Pastor of what had been dubbed by the statisticians as the "fastest growing" church in the country. I have preached all over the country, written motivational books, spoken for universities, sat with dignitaries all over the world. I was a celebrated author with fairly strong influence in this country and abroad. I didn't have to take it. Surely, I could pick up the phone and straighten this out. Well, I tried just that. But it didn't help.

One night after a great service with a tremendously strong anointing on me, I went straight to the hospital. I threw her covers back and prayed the fervent prayer of a seasoned prayer veteran. I had seen God heal countless people through my hands. Why not my own mother? I spoke the Word, I stood on His promise, and finally I sobbed on the pillow. Yes, I prayed the prayer of faith; she smiled at me, kissed me, and went to sleep with food still in her mouth. My raw heart ached.

THE POWER OF PATIENCE

These are the times that try our hearts beyond what we could ever imagine for ourselves. The times that are the most exasperating are the times when all human efforts fail. We become powerless. The human arms have been stretched to their limit. The legs are spent, the face strained, and there is no relief. The times that challenge your faith are those times when all you know about God doesn't assist you in getting results, and heaven seems closed for the evening. But I learned some things about God's silence. I had spent my life learning His Word, but I had never been taught about God's silence. Whenever He doesn't speak a word, He is teaching even in the stillness. Allowing His students to derive implicit conclusions requires the hushed smile and watchful eye of a wise teacher. God said nothing at all. He waited, and after much protesting, so did I.

Somewhere in the storm, somewhere in the salty, blinding tears of struggle, I found a friend. I had fought the disease, denied the evidence, wept inwardly over the symptoms. I had made countless phone calls getting information and options. I wanted to fly her to the best possible care. I had told her physicians, "Let's send her to Paris or some place where she can get some experimental miracle drug." I was willing to sell my house to save my mother. I got the best possible doctors, but the best didn't help.

But gradually, the whispers of a friend called Patience calmed my racing heart. Patience is what God gives you when bad things remain unchanged; it is the fiery furnace that forges an eternal Hope. Patience is what He teaches in His silence. Faith comes by hearing, but patience comes only by absolute silence.

And not only so, but we glory in tribulations also: knowing that tribulation worketh patience. (Romans 5:3, KJV)

Sometimes you can't go on without patience. It is what enables the distance runner not to collapse from fatigue. If the trial is going to be a long one, we all must learn to run with patience. Do not run without patience. It is God's sedative for the tormented soul. Patience is the balm that God rubs into the aching muscles when the soul is being stretched and the race must still be run. There are moments, my friend, when tribulations last so long that only God can release the patience, the sheer grace to sustain you. And finally the inner hysteria stops, and you settle down and realize that it will take as long as it takes.

This experience was my trainer sent to get me in shape. There are some races you have to run even when you are exhausted. Either you get bitter about life and quit, or you get better and endure. God teaches you patience for the soul by allowing you to push yourself. This resistance in your life is just an opportunity to stretch. It is here that He teaches us to overcome our feelings and pursue our goals ignoring the pain. Pursuing and moving forward and, oh yes, forever just waiting.

FINAL LESSONS

I rearranged my life to accommodate my mom. I accepted that there were some hindrances that would not be easily overcome. For a while, my mother was much better. Her brain healed and her scars were barely traceable. Momentarily, we won the battle; we snatched her back from death's door. But like all those who were healed or even resurrected in the Bible, they were raised to die again. My mother finally succumbed to the ultimate peace of the Lord even before I could finish this chapter.

Despite the many stretching expectations of losing her, I still ache inside terribly and miss her. I could never imagine my life without her and now I am forced to. But the tribulations of her extended illness have been a genuine gift from God through the love she and I shared. Caring for her, loving her, suffering with her, they have all shown me what it means to sacrifice oneself for another. To taste the palpable texture of love so sharp and sweet that it burns the throat.

> For this is My commandment, that you love one another as I have loved you. Greater love has no one than this, than to lay down one's life for his friends. (John 15:12–13, NKJV)

The transition from life unto death is part of our existence. For these things are the cycles of life, too long enforced to be overturned by someone as weak as you and I. Only Christ rose to die no more. The rest of us are just waiting. And while we wait, we must maximize these few brief shining moments, and then suddenly or gradually we will all go away.

And so we turn another corner, and we stride another lap. The soul stretches, the emotions flare, the cycles that have gone on from Adam and Eve until now continue to perpetuate themselves. This is a long race from Adam to me. I had better calm down if I am going to make the long haul. How about you?

Is God still good? Of course He is. I have learned that He is there in the race with you—coaching you, teaching you, and sometimes even carrying you. He allows my soul to be stretched like everyone else's. It is just that He uses different things with different people. All of us will face something that stretches our soul until it is taut and strained. It is there at the point of strain that we find patience and a clearer view of God's grace.

I pushed against my mother's passing with all of my might, but it didn't move. I grunted, screamed, prayed, and cried but all to no avail. And then finally, I wrapped my big strong arms around my frail trembling mother and continued the process of life. You see, when we are children our parents carry our small frames up the stairs and put our exhausted bodies to bed until the morning. Little did I know then that one day when we are older, we will carry their frail bodies like they did ours and put them to bed until the morning. I am glad for strong arms, thankful that her bed is made and the room is warm. It was my privilege to carry the dear lady from my arms back to the God who gave her to me.

At about nine-thirty in the evening, I kissed her face and wished her goodnight. She died in my arms, surrounded by her children. The great educator who graduated from university on the dean's list and taught hundreds of children, the matriarch of our family, taught us one final lesson. She taught us how to live and now she taught us how to die. I can still hear her final sigh, her final breath as it blew by my ear. She had reached her final destination, and all I could say was, "Goodnight, Momma. I'll see you in the morning."

Tomorrow my children will say goodnight to me, and so the race goes on and on and on. And even in the blinding rain, the sun shines through and crystallizes our tears into beautiful diamonds that glisten while we remain in shadowed light for just a little while.

EXPECTATION LIMITATION

My painful journey leading to the loss of my mother in this life is just one example of soul stretching. It is one example of the many things that we push and push against with our fierce faith and tenacious will and see little results, and then silently, so silently, we wonder, "Why?" Great effort doesn't always mean great results. Sometimes faith is perfected more when things do not change than when they do. You do not need hope for what you can see, or faith for what you have attained. You need faith when no answer comes. You need faith when life makes no sense. You need faith when you can't explain why the baby dies, why the job falls through, why the marriage isn't working, why the wicked prosper, the good die, the righteous suffer, and the kind receive no comfort.

Often when we cannot understand life's circumstances with our limited human perspective, we also limit our expectations of who God is and what He can do. We think there is only one good outcome—the one we want! Instead, we need to trust our Father, for He may have even bigger things in mind. We must try to see Him at work in whatever trials come our way. We must remember that God's expectations are bigger than our own. We experience the expectation limitation of not believing that we can run the race to its conclusion.

When my mother passed away, some well-intended folks offered me canned clichés and kind remarks about her new home in Heaven. I know that they were trying to comfort me, but like an old lady stumbling along the road, comfort walks slowly and often dawdles along the way. Comfort comes in its own good time, and that is okay because sometimes we need to allow time for the stretched muscle to heal.

My ligaments are torn, my heart breaks, my soul aches, but that is all part of the process. The pain is indicative of how strenuous the workout was, how precious the gift, and how deep the loss. I know that God knows when to stretch what. In the days to come, a greater agility will result from this stretching. The muscle will become stronger. As the healing progresses, there will be days that I will wince with painful reminders of the loss, but this soreness will reinforce the truth that no one becomes a great runner without being stretched beyond what they think they can handle.

The spectators that sit in the stands will not know of this stretching. They will see the swift limbs, the flailing arms, and stomping feet that lurch across the finish line. They will comment on the quick gait and strong legs, but they will not know that the runner can leap over hurdles and hurl himself down the track because he was hit hard and has endured the painful, private stretching of the soul. As the old gospel song declares, he has come this far by faith.

Faith is not always an instrument of change. Sometimes it is a means of survival. Sometimes faith gives you patience to trust God when His will collides with our loves and we are left holding a wilted rose and packing boxes filled with nightgowns from the long night when we put our mother to bed. The crowd will not know that behind the track we were stretched beyond description so that we could run our race. All we can do is run and have faith.

Are you in the throws of some strenuous struggle? Are you being stretched beyond former limits even as you read this? Parents, children, finances, or whatever it may be, the details vary, but the workout is still the same. Let me make some suggestions about how to appropriate hope and transcend your present expectations. Inhale slowly, fill your lungs, and take a deep breath. Exhale slowly: Allow the weight of the trial to work through your thoughts, fears, and, if necessary, your tears. Lamenting relieves the soul like the exhaling of carbon dioxide. Just because the soul weeps doesn't mean it is dying. Feel the ligaments of your soul stretch.

And don't believe that it's a one-time process either. Don't think to yourself, "Oh, I've stretched now, so I can go on quickly to better times." Waves of grief will come like the mighty sea throws its current at the beach. It will come and go, but you must persevere step by step. Whatever you do, don't drown in your own pool of grief. Visit it if you must, dip your feet in, and bathe in it, but do not stop there and allow yourself to be pulled under the current.

How do we avoid the ferocious riptide of sorrow that seeks to suck all hope out of our lives? Oddly enough, we need to feel the grief without tying it around our necks. Let it land on our shoulders, but do not anchor your heart to its talons. Run on, my friend, past that stage to the next. Experience the full range of emotions that come from the strength to strain and then give in to the realities while challenging the possibilities. Indulge yourself in those rare moments of laughter that come even in the face of death or danger. It is amazing that even a grief-stricken family can laugh at times. Take full advantage of those times and drink them in like water for the parched soul. All of us will go jogging through the dry place of great challenge. Laughter helps the soul to medicate and alleviate the tension of those times. Most comedians have come from great brokenness and sadness. They survived by watering the soul, keeping it moist with laughter, until they just learned to run on. Being able to find the comic even amongst the ruins of tragedy also stretches the limitations of our expectations. It requires us to step outside of the present pain and adjust focus. This in itself is a healing balm. The sage reminds us of this in Proverbs when he writes, "A cheerful heart is good medicine, but a crushed spirit dries up the bones" (17:22, NIV).

CROSS TRAINING

Balance is the key word in the race. Avoid extremes, stay in the middle of the road. Especially during the rigors of a trial, we must commit ourselves to the consistent behaviors that help us endure. Marathon runners do not wake up one morning and decide to run for thirty miles. They trained and trained and trained some more. You may have heard the popular term "cross-training." This approach encourages athletes to work different muscle groups and participate in different sports in order to enhance their performance in their own particular competition. In the race for our life's goals, we are called to a different kind of cross-training; we are called to the task of picking up our crosses daily and trusting that if we remain faithful in the little things, God will see us through the next step.

Our cross-training has practical components, too. We should practice the behaviors that we know to be beneficial to us: daily time in prayer, maintaining morals, caring for each other. Too often, when we suffer the lashes from an ongoing tribulation, we use our pain as an excuse to become a spiritual couch potato. We justify sinful pleasures because we hurt so much. Although we may have moments when our legs go weak and our knees buckle, we must remain faithful and run the course before us. We do this by focusing on each step, each stride, each lap, on the moment of the next breath, and not on the overwhelming miles before us.

I have had my moments, as I am sure you have also, and I haven't always cross-trained the way I know I should. But at last, my muscles are relaxing, my perspectives altering, and I am loose enough to run with patience the course that God has set for me to run. You learn that when trouble persists long enough, you begin to accept what you cannot control and control with all diligence what you can. There are some variables in any storm that you can control. They are the moving parts of life.

And usually, that is all we can do, anyway—move the parts of life that are moveable and then respond proficiently to the things that seem as inflexible as a concrete wall. God eventually moves them. Sometimes the natural progression of life removes them. But by then patience has stirred her perfect work in your heart, and you have learned to calmly pace yourself for the long-distance run.

In order to maintain our stride, I've found it helpful to remember two important things in the midst of these troubles. First, although we are powerless over some things, we are not powerless over all things. We have a choice about how we respond in the face of adversity. We can choose to quit the race altogether, leaving the track by way of the self-ish shortcuts of denial, addiction, or betrayal. But, my friend, if you want to run the race that God has set before you, then stay on the track. The path is dark, narrow, and steep at times, but He provides enough light to let us see the next step before us.

The second lesson is that we must see these trials as opportunities to fulfill God's work. It may seem like we're working our own way through these trials, but the truth is that we are glorifying our King and becoming more like the perfect example of His Son. The only reason why we would want to jump off the track and abandon our painful journey is because we're momentarily confused about what fulfills us. In the intense, gut-wrenching valleys of life, we succumb to the temptation that what we really crave is convenience, comfort, and materialism. These are the same tricks that Satan used to tempt our Lord after His forty days of fasting in the desert. But like Jesus, we must not succumb to the illusory temptations of the Enemy. We must remember that only our Father and His purposes, no matter how painful they may seem at the moment, truly satisfy our souls.

WIND BENEATH OUR WINGS

Our stories are not over. The problems are not all resolved. But I believe that the hurdles stand in the road as milestones to cross. After the leaping, gaping challenges are crossed, we must keep the hurdles as the trophies of life. They decorate my heart with the friendly reminder that things eventually work out. Even the things that I thought would kill me only stretched me until I developed the limber, relaxed posture of a patient man who walks, runs and, occasionally, crawls with God.

What a paradox the race of life is when we think about it. God tells us that we are to run with patience. We come back to our original question about this imperative: How can we run, which implies to hurry, and still have patience, which implies to remain calm? I believe the key is to embrace the stretching, continue moving, and trust that God will provide us with strength and endurance beyond what we can imagine. In His Word, this process emerges in one of the most beautiful images throughout all Scripture:

> *But those who wait on the Lord shall renew their strength; they shall mount up with wings like eagles, they shall run and not be weary, they shall walk and not be faint. (Isaiah 40:31, NKJV)*

God created us to be resilient if we rely on Him and exercise our faith as we run. He renews those who are weary and exhausted from the arduous journeys and rocky pitfalls of life. I like the way the prophet Isaiah here mixes the metaphor between flying and running. Those times when we feel like we are too tired to run, walk, or even crawl, He carries us and sustains us. He gives us wings of faith on which to fly. He becomes the wind beneath our wings.

We do our part and our Lord does His, however silent He may seem in the moment. Once again, it's the tension between doing and being, running and being calm. It seems odd, but any runner will tell you that a good long-distance sprinter has to move his body with speed but his breathing must remain calm, steady, focused. If you are going to run, you can't get too excited because the anxiety will cut off your wind. Sometimes you just have to steady your pace and face your life. You cannot fix everything. You will push against some things, and they will not move. When they do not move, just remember that He is stretching you, that you will be renewed with wings like eagles. Calm yourself, steady your course, relinquish your fears, don't dwell on the past or worry about the future. Just lift your head up and keep your back straight and run with patience the race that is set before you. Feel the wind of His breath beneath your wings and soar beyond your own expectations!

EIGHT

HEARING VOICES

Sounds are all around us. Rarely do we find ourselves, even in the quietest of spots, truly bathed in silence. This morning as I write this, my office is a quiet place, but nonetheless I can still hear the chirp of a cricket somewhere outside my door, the drone of a lawnmower trimming the last emerald blades of summer, the dull roar of a jet passing overhead. Occasionally, familiar voices from down the hall filter through my ears, causing me to pause and catch snatches of words, phrases, and laughter.

Inside my head, various voices echo and reverberate like the shouts of hikers across a canyon. Don't get me wrong; it's not that I have multiple personalities yelling back and forth at each other inside me. No, it's simply the cacophony of voices inside each of us that blends into the conscious thought-stream of who we are. One voice inside me is thinking about my schedule this day: the meetings I'm supposed to attend, the appointments to keep, the services I will lead and preach at tonight. Another voice is reminding me to call my wife, to let her know how much I love her even in the midst of a busy day. Yet another is concentrating on what to say in the words that I am writing on the page. There's even a hisslike voice saying, "You'll never get everything done today. You might as well not try. Nothing you do makes a difference anyway."

Now, like I said, please don't think I'm crazy because I'm hearing voices both inside and outside my head. We all do. It's part of who we are and the way we are conditioned. These voices obviously impact how we learn to maximize our moments. When we listen to the bitter words that spring up like bile, we are likely to fail, to give up, to settle for so much less than we're called to. When we learn to filter out the unnecessary critical voices, then we start to listen to the powerful, confident song pulling us forward. The problem comes, of course, when we do not assess what we're hearing and try to listen to each and every one. The real problem comes when we listen to the wrong voices and begin believing them even though we know they are the seductive lies of defeat. Then we act on them and sabotage our inner dreams and capabilities.

In order to master our moments so that we may maximize them, we must assess the variety of voices within our lives, both around us and inside us, and learn how to control our responses to each sound that we hear. We must examine the shrill chorus of criticism alongside the sweet music of encouragement and assess the dance we do to each. We will discover that there are numerous voices both outside of us and within us that either contribute to our downfall with an "I-told-you-so" smirk or else contribute to our triumph with a whisper of "You can do it" as we turn the next lap. The trick, of course, is knowing how to respond to each one.

SINNER OR SAINT

Some years ago my good friend Bishop Eddie Long and I were on our way to an appointment. Walking down the street in downtown Atlanta, we saw a lady dressed in shabby, tattered clothes standing on the curb preaching in a particularly boisterous fashion. We continued to walk forward and soon she was right in front of us. She was so engrossed in her message of hellfire and brimstone that she seemed not to notice us. We continued toward our appointment, and as we passed her she screamed, "I see you no-good stinking preachers! Come out of you Eiffel Towers for a minute, didn't you? What are you doing down here? Thought I didn't know who you was? Everybody knows you no-good stinking preachers!" I was shocked, but I said nothing and neither did Bishop Long. We thought it best not to escalate the situation by responding to her deranged screaming. I was amazed that someone who didn't know us could say such hideous things about us. Anyone who knew us would know that, beyond pulpit ministry, both of us minister to the homeless, the hurting, drug addicts and anyone else in need. Both of us have adult education programs for inner-city, at-risk people who receive assistance from our churches.

Her attack lacked logic. We were attacked through a stereotypical prejudice. I am always shocked when intelligent people say they do not like someone they don't even know. But if you listen, people do it all the time. They jump to conclusions and then crank up the volume without considering the impact on those around them.

As we continued further down the street, I could still hear her screaming obscenely behind us. We weren't a complete block away when a young man leaning against a wall looked up and saw us. His eyes filled with tears, and he opened his mouth and started saying loudly, "These are some great men of God! These men changed my life." I smiled at him but continued walking. I was sure he didn't hear the insults we had just received. I was glad he didn't. I could see the riot that might have broken out between him and the lady, who was probably still screaming down on the corner.

As I walked away, I thought how amazing it was that in the space of one block someone had all but called us devils, and someone else had all but called us saints. Yet neither of them added nor detracted from who we really were. All we had to do to progress was just keep walking. I am not comparing us to Jesus, but I couldn't help thinking of a similar situation in His life. One moment, the people said crown him, and the next they cried crucify him. In the midst of life, we must keep walking through opposing opinions. Whether you are Princess Diana, a secular hero to many, or you are Martin Luther King, Jr., a saintly crusader to others, you will always hear both voices on the same street. The secret to achieving success is to always just keep on walking, no matter what you hear!

CRIES OF CRITICISM

The loudest and most boisterous of the external voices that we must quell comes from the Critics, that contingency of sharp-edged vipers who could find fault with anyone. Non-constructive Critics are nitpickers, those who miss out on the beauty of the orchard because they are so obsessed with the wormhole they found in one apple. These judgmental fruit-inspectors will always find something to harp about and criticize whatever we do, however we do it. Keep in mind, my friend, that I'm not talking about the constructive blows from friends or critics who desire your good. We will discuss them later. Nor am I talking about the illogical attacks from peripheral people in our lives like the old woman who berated me and Bishop Long.

No, critics know us well, but they usually do not care about us or our well-being. The discordant din of discouragement from the Critics is based on their envy, jealousy, and discontent. In fact, their criticism may actually have nothing to do with you at all. They simply feel cheated by life and rather than take control of their heart's dreams, they would rather squelch other people's hopes in an attempt to drag them down into the squalor of despair with them.

Now, while it's tempting to want to retaliate and return their cruel critiques with our own observations concerning their weaknesses and failures, that is not the example our Lord set for us. Nor is it the high road to success that we are seeking in order to maximize our lives. Trading barbs with this bunch of nitpickers is like becoming a tennis ball at Wimbledon: back and forth, back and forth you go, with no one the winner because your heart ends up volleyed out of bounds. So how do we respond?

You have heard that it was said, "Eye for eye, and tooth for tooth." But I tell you, Do not resist an evil person. If someone strikes you on the right cheek, turn to him the other also. (Matthew 5:38–39, NIV)

Do not repay anyone evil for evil. Be careful to do what is right in the eyes of everybody. If it is possible, as far as it depends on you, live at peace with everybody. (Romans 12:17–18, NIV)

We turn the other cheek. As humbling and painful as it may be, we should simply heap burning coals on the heads of these sharp-tongued destructors by allowing them their say and then going on with our journeys. Do not let them get under your skin. They are not worth your time to sit and stew about. Simply listen to them, thank them, and take their criticism with a grain of salt. Save your time and reflective energies for those wise critics whom you trust, that band of men and women who loves you enough to tell you the truth, even when it hurts.

TONGUES OF DECEIT

Before we examine the voices of those helpful critics, let's single out another pervasive voice that we must all confront from time to time. They are not the loud, raucous Critics who usually reveal their intent right off the bat. No, the voice of this kind of person is as smooth and sweet as honey dripping off the fresh amber comb. These voices are often easy to listen to because they tell us what we would like to hear: "You're the best speaker I've ever heard!" "You are such a beautiful woman." "I wish I were as talented as you are." "How do you manage to do all you do? You're a regular Superman!" And on and on the sweet notes of flattery drip off the tongues of Deceivers and into our hungry ears.

It's not that I don't trust someone just because they flatter me. No, it's just that I'm wary of the voice that consistently inflates me so that when my bubble bursts, the pop echoes louder. The Deceivers flatter you and then eventually reveal a hidden agenda. They butter you up like a piece of dry toast before taking quick bites from your soul. They pretend to want your best but eventually transform their charm into a self-serving pied piper's tune, leading you away from your true identity and your true mission toward a dangerous precipice of deceptive illusion.

Lead me, O Lord, in your righteousness because of my enemies—make straight your way before me. Not a word from their mouth can be trusted; their throat is an open grave; with their tongue they speak deceit. (Psalm 5:8–9, NIV)

These yes-men, who tell us what we want to hear just to get whatever they want from us, are nothing more than false encouragers. In many ways, it is easier to dispel the Critics than these crafty charlatans because the Critics are much more blatant and up-front about what they're doing. The Deceivers, on the other hand, are dressed in the camouflage fatigues of compliments and kiss-ups. They know how to spot our weakness and use it against us in the most subtle ways. They know how to play mind games and simply insinuate some flaw or criticism and let our own internal critical voices do the rest.

Obviously, we should be on guard against these people and avoid succumbing to their sticky webs. But, unfortunately, we do not always know who the Deceivers are until it's too late, after they have betrayed us, after their true intentions have emerged and we are left to pick up the pieces of our shattered trust. For me, the best antidote against the allure of the Deceivers is to remain humble before the Lord and others. I must never regard myself as higher or lower than I really am; this way, I remove the power of any compliments to fulfill me more than they should. I find that I must never regard flattery as anything more than a quick, cool wind on a hot day. It relieves the heat momentarily, but the hard work of the rest of the day remains. Try to accept the compliments that come your way as graciously as you can. At the same time, do not elevate yourself to a position of superiority because of the elevated language of some admirer. Take the time to discover if the ones flattering you are indeed trustworthy. If they prove themselves, then perhaps you can elevate them to the group of wise, trusted, beloved individuals who you count among the true friends that God has gifted your way. If not, then try and learn from the failed relationship and be on guard the next time the compliments flow like wine at the wedding in Cana.

THE PEANUT GALLERY

The final category of destructive voices is filled with what I call the Peanut Gallery, the collection of spectators who think they know better than we do what we should be doing and how to do it. The problem is that they usually know nothing about the topic. Like an arm-chair quarterback who has never picked up a football, or a backseat driver who has never gripped a steering wheel, these voices attempt to instruct or correct without having any experience whatsoever of who we are. These people are simply not close enough to us to have credibility, authority, or say-so in our lives. We should simply ignore them.

Without being rude or deliberately unkind, we must press on toward our goal and let the Peanut Gallery stand along the side lines and watch the game. These folks may be too scared to suit up and run onto the field, or they may lack the talent and faith to persevere. They may be unwilling to live out the God-given role placed before them because they are too envious of your position and the accomplishments of others. Consequently, they are on the lookout for opportunities to shoot down those soaring upon the horizon in front of them—you who are trying to live out your best and mount up with wings like eagles.

The tongue of the wise commends knowledge, but the mouth of the fool gushes folly. (Proverbs 15:2, NIV)

Do not speak to a fool, for he will scorn the wisdom of your words. (Proverbs 23:9, NIV)

Like the extreme voices that I heard as I strolled down the street in Atlanta, comments from these acquaintances should never be given the power to upset or elate us. That power is reserved for the final category of voices, the power of language from a loving heart directed toward fueling our journey by its kindness, encouragement, or challenge.

CHORUS OF ENCOURAGERS

Think back on the faces of those who stand along the shoulders of the road you have traveled. Who has constantly cheered you on as you dashed down the lane? Who has yelled and whooped and hollered in celebration as you reached those milestones of accomplishment? Who has whispered words of comfort and healing when you have fallen and felt like you simply could not get back on your feet again? Look into their eyes. There's the grade-school teacher who gave you the belief in yourself to keep going, even when the math problem seemed too hard. There's the coach who pushed you to your limit as your lungs burned and your legs trembled from the exhaustion of wind sprints. There stands the boss who believed in your talents enough to give you the extra responsibilities that led to your promotion. Always, always, there are the voices of our mother and father patiently encouraging us in our life's journey. There are the songs of our siblings, the sweet breath of children, the tunes of our friends, the lyrics of all those dear people, alive and dead, who have joined in the chorus of Encouragers who have sustained us on our journeys thus far.

Give great thanks to our Almighty for these precious people who saw your potential when you could not see it yourself, who did not give up on you when you wanted to give up on yourself. For the folks who are still part of your life today, tell them how much they mean. Write them a note, send them a card, or surprise them with flowers. They are the ones who will continue to provide the music of your soul. They are the ones to whom you should attune your radio receiver and to whom you should listen carefully and thoughtfully.

Their encouraging words and uplifting voices do not exclude criticism or harshness at times, for if someone really loves us, they will have to point out the shortcomings in our lives, the sinfulness, and the areas that need improvement. We may be tempted to dismiss them as malicious Critics or dangerous Deceivers, but if we honestly consider the sting of their words and find truth, not venom, in their message, then we must listen. If we sense the love in their quavering tone, the love for us that is willing to risk how we may respond to them based on their harsh words, then we must listen.

> *Open rebuke is better than love carefully concealed. Faithful are the wounds of a friend, but the kisses of an enemy are deceitful. (Proverbs 27:5–6, NKJV)*

The truth sometimes hurts, my friend. But you must have faith that the Encouragers in your life really do have your best interests at heart. If you are going to experience any sense of accomplishment in this life, you must have someone around you whom you can trust, someone who can help you to see where you are.

It is difficult to find someone who is confident enough to tell you who you are and where you are without becoming jealous or insecure about what they see. As we have seen, there is certainly an endless abundance of spiteful nay-sayers along with the parade of yes-men, who always bestow flowery compliments even when they are not applicable or accurate. Every leader needs someone he or she can ask, when the stage lights are out and the work is done, "Who do you say that I am?"

> *And Jesus went out, and his disciples, into the towns of Caesarea Philippi: and by the way he asked his disciples, saying unto them, Whom do men say that I am? And they answered, John the Baptist: but some say, Elias; and others, One of the prophets. And he saith unto them, But whom say ye that I am? And Peter answereth and saith unto him, Thou art the Christ. (Mark 8:27–29, KJV)*

If we are to know ourselves and know how we come across to others, then we must have trustworthy Encouragers who are committed to telling us the truth, not what we want to hear and not a response fueled by jealousy or spite. Love these dear people by trying to return the wise counsel and serving them with the same challenge of your vision for who they are ultimately called to be.

MINNOWS IN A STREAM

Have you ever stopped to consider all of the voices that make you who you are? At any given moment, a variety of ideas darts through your mind like minnows released into the clear crystal waters of a meadow pond. They dash in every direction, colliding, bouncing, usually going their separate ways. They flow into that stream-of-consciousness that determines who we are and how we behave. If we do not get the minnows flowing in the same direction most of the time, then they, too, have the power to continually distract us and keep us from fulfilling our life's goal. Not one of those little fish-ideas can grow into the big fish-goal it wants to be unless we monitor and provide a net for our thoughts, fears, and dreams.

One of the first voices that develops in our heads is the responsible, dutiful voice that reminds us who we are and what we are called to. It expects us to live up to a high standard, but at the same time, it knows we are human and tries to be patient and gracious with us when we fail or forget something. This voice is comparable to the ego in psychological personality development. We should try to cultivate a healthy harmony within this voice and listen to its consistent, rhythmic beat each day. It is the one that most people hear when they meet us and we interact with them.

This internal voice provides many positives: a consistent tune for the dance of each day. It is the one which is trying to make things happen, to keep you on time with your schedule, juggling the demands of your day, telling you to hurry up. It's good because it directs the inner traffic.

Another voice that we often hear is the silly, sarcastic voice that wants to comment on everything, make a joke out of everything, and take the day off. Like a little child who is usually cooped up inside the schoolroom and then suddenly released to the playground, this voice must have some fun or it can turn destructive. This voice must not be neglected or ignored, but you certainly cannot live every day as if you're ten years old when you're thirty or forty or more.

When we strive too far toward perfection and an unattainable standard, then we have shifted into the realm of the internal critic. This voice is rarely pleased. While it can become a healthy duet partner for the sillier, childlike voice within us, it can also become the strict, abusive parent who may mean well but who ends up using too harsh a force nonetheless. We have to learn to hold ourselves accountable, to think through the morality of what we're doing and saying. But we must also be willing to forgive ourselves and move on to a new tune instead of warping the record by playing it over and over and over again.

The key to successful living is to try to keep these internal voices in balance, to help them help each other by allowing each one to contribute its positives and to make its criticisms constructive. Don't allow one to sing solo for too long while the others are stuck in the dim shadows as back-up singers. Give them each a turn to sing as a united, harmonious trio, committed to the fulfillment of your glorious destiny.

PITCHFORKS AND HALOS

Ultimately, the most powerful voices we will hear within us are the voices of good and evil: the soft, silent words of the Holy Spirit instructing our heart or the stinging rebukes and oil-smooth temptations from the greatest Deceiver of them all. We must be especially attuned to each of these and know how to respond to each in order to succeed and continue on our journey successfully. We must know how to tune out the Evil One and resist his schemes. We must know how to focus on the presence of the Spirit within us and the language of longing He is inscribing on our hearts.

Do you remember the old television commercial that was used to describe internal conflicts? A man had two little men riding one on each shoulder. One of the little men was dressed in white and wore a halo on his head. He was the voice of good telling the man the "right choice." On the other shoulder was perched a red-suited, pitchfork-carrying ghoul with a tail. He, of course, was the symbol of evil. They both were struggling to gain influence in the life of the poor guy who was stuck in the middle. That rather humorous illustration may not be as humorous as we thought. If truth be told, we must be prepared to deal with those two inner voices every day. The key to success is knowing which voice to listen to.

IN THE PRESENCE OF EVIL

Have you ever pursued a goal and in the midst of preparing it there was a red-suited demon screaming in your ears, saying, "Are you a fool? You must be out of your mind. You can't do this. You are not capable. You are absolutely incompetent. Those little accomplishments you had before were just luck. You were at the right place at the right time and you made it, but you better know that you can't do this. This deal is too big for you. You are in over your head. You are going to make a public spectacle out of yourself. You are shooting too high"? And on and on and on it goes. This voice will wake you in the middle of the night. It comes complete with a bitter taste of bile and the trembling shudders of fear. This is the voice that comes like a cancer to erode your self-perception and limit your faith in yourself.

The voice of evil will be there to suggest incompetence. This voice exists in every boardroom, bedroom, closet, and along every sidewalk of this world. It is an evil voice; it doesn't play fair. It plays on your deepest fears and basest frailties, past failures, insecurities, and inhibitions.

SYMPHONY OF HEAVEN

The only way to overcome this evil voice is to become caught up in the music within your heart. God speaks to us in the still, small altar of our hearts and sends His Spirit to remain in us and with us as His children. While it may seem so easy to succumb to the bubble-gum rap of the devil, with its catchy rhythm and clever lyrics, the symphony of heaven is more refined. It requires more experience to fully appreciate and appropriate. It is a sophisticated blend of numerous events, instruments, and musicians coming together to remind us of who we are and what our destiny is.

When we attune our ears to this glorious, melodious voice, it is not as if all our problems are solved or as if all the other voices forever fade away. No, instead, it is like the feeling of having an intimate conversation in a busy, bustling, crowded place. Have you ever tried to do that? Perhaps you were catching up with an old friend or seeing a loved one off at the train station or airport. There are thousands of sounds surrounding the two of you: loudspeakers, children crying, televisions blaring, cups and saucers clinking, wheels rolling, footsteps falling, and on and on. But you're not listening to all of those sounds because you are so focused on the sound of your friend's voice, on the inflection in her words, or the cadence in his lilting speech. We become oblivious to the hundreds of distractions around us because we are so focused on someone we care about and delight in.

It is the same with the voice of God and His ongoing words of life to us. Whether He is speaking through His Scripture, through other of His children, or through our life circumstances, He is always communicating with a heart that seeks Him. As we discussed in the last chapter, He even finds a way to communicate with us in His apparent silence.

MIX MASTER

These days, composing is computerized. Precision instruments and mixing boards allow for the production of musical masterpieces. With mixing boards, each component of the composition is recorded on a separate track. Vocalist, guitarist, keyboard player, drummer are all recorded separately and then the tracks are mixed to put the song together. The advantage of this system is that each track can be altered without affecting the performance of the other participants. The production specialist can bring the horns up or the violin down with a simple touch of his hand.

The technician in the studio is just as important as the performers on the stage. You see, if the music is not mixed correctly, the blend of sound can be discordant and painful to listen to. You have to be the technician of your life and mix the various voices you hear in the studio of your mind. You cannot allow negative voices to have as much volume as does the sweet voice of you Savior, who has promised to sustain you. You have to isolate bad tracks, narrow opinions, and critical dispositions, not allowing them to spin the composition of your life.

> Finally, brothers, whatever is true, whatever is noble, whatever is right, whatever is pure, whatever is lovely, whatever is admirable—if anything is excellent or praiseworthy—think about such things. (Philippians 4:8, NIV)

You may have to turn down some voices and focus on the tracks that are good. If you can do that, your mix will be so effective that others will hear and enjoy the excellence of your harmonious life. This ability to be a mix master enables you to create concerts out of chaos.

Sometimes there will be rhythmic drumming of impending dangers. Often we will contend with the heart-thumping bass notes of tempestuous peril. But these sounds should not dominate the greater melody of a calm and successful composition created by keeping everything in its proper perspective. As I said earlier, you must keep walking past your detractors and your distractions and make the music in your heart what you need and want to hear. Do this and watch others listen to the surround sound that emanates from the heart of a well-adjusted person who knows how to master the mix and create a sweet, sweet sound.

Part Three

MAXIMIZE THE MOMENT

NINE

───◦◊◦───

A PLACE
CALLED "THERE"

There is a place called "there." It is not a neighborhood one lives in. You can't find it on a map. Neither money, nor education, nor influence can get you there. It is a place in life that all wise people seek. It is the place where your soul starts to sing, the place that you sense with all that is in you: "This is where I am meant to be!" "There" is the place that God calls us to from the beginning, and most of us spend years, like rats in a maze, trying to make it through all the twists and turns of life to get "there."

It appears that "there" is the answer to the test of time. The object of the game of life is to get "there" before the bell rings. So we run, sometimes wildly, often chaotically, trying desperately to attain a place so difficult to articulate that most people do not understand what drives us. Like children playing tag, we get touched by this place called "there," and then run and search, trying to find this place. Yes, once you have been touched by destiny, it evades you and almost avoids you. Yet it teases you, taunts you, flirtingly allures you. Tag, you are it! Get up and go after it before the bell rings and the game ends and you find that you wasted your time missing what could have been mastered; calling what could have been conquered; and hoping for what could have been had.

WHERE IS "THERE"?

Sometimes all you have to go on is a very poor description of how to proceed. It feels like life hands you a warrant for the arrest of the place called "there." You are trying to apprehend this villain without an adequate description of who or where he is. There are few witnesses to assist you because most have given up their search and settled for some poor consolation prize. But there are a few of us who will not be denied. Our nostrils have been touched by the scent, are hot on the trail, and until we find "there," we will have no peace. In fact, for us, water isn't wet without it; grass doesn't seem green; colors lose their brilliance and the sun loses its heat. We must have it. We are bounty hunters, and the bounty is the titillating sensation that comes from sitting down in the proverbial rocking chair and saying to yourself, "I have been 'there' and done that."

Getting "there" is a feeling. It is what makes a true teacher teach. It is what makes a true actor act or a true preacher preach. It is what compels the chemical engineer to pursue his craft. It is what makes the astronaut look into the stars. It is the passion that burns within you like a flaming torch. When you get "there," you will know it in the deepest part of your soul.

WHERE ART THOU?

And the LORD God called unto Adam, and said unto him, Where art thou? (Genesis 3:9, KJV)

It doesn't matter where "there" is for you, it just matters that you get there. It matters that you achieve soul satisfaction. It matters that you reach your full purpose and potential. It matters that you attain your highest and best use. If you sense as you read this that you're not "there," that's okay. There is no harm in not being "there" if you are on your way, if you're in hot pursuit, in the process of journeying to a place called "there." The real tragedy is when you're not even going in the right direction. It means you're lost. It means you have spent many days, months, or even years, which you cannot reclaim, and you haven't even begun the real journey.

But the good news is that if you realize that you have been running in circles, you can stop and make today, right now, a starting place. Every journey must start somewhere, and the time is now if you are not already on your way. Remember that setbacks are really setups for you to come forward and reassess where you are and where you are going. Recently, while in a large urban mall, I looked at the directory of stores and services. There was a chart showing each level of the mall's floor plan. It had all of the stores, restaurants, and sites in the mall neatly mapped out. There was a red arrow pointing to the very spot where I was standing. Beside the point were the words, "You are here." You see, the mall managers know that if you can't figure out where you are, you will never know where you are going. They know that modern shoppers are often in a hurry and want to know the most direct route to their favorite store rather than wandering around aimlessly, hoping to find it accidentally. We must assess our present position if we are to move forward to "there."

Perhaps that is why God called Adam in the garden by saying, "Where art thou?" In other words, do you know where you are? Of course Adam knew he was hiding; he later says so. But does he know that he has stepped out of the place called "there"? That was all that mattered to God. He had made a move that had compromised his destination. Redirection begins with admission and then confrontation. You must admit where you are and then confront what mishaps brought

you to the wrong destination in life. Did I say destination? I am sorry—
I should have said station. It is not a destination if you don't stop!

LIVING OVER "THERE"

You are the most effective when you are operating in a "there" state of
being. Countless people have found their "there." They found it and we
felt it. Men and women like Nelson Mandela, Mother Teresa, Martin
Luther King, Jr., George Washington Carver, Helen Keller, Mozart,
Thomas Edison, Michelangelo, Walt Whitman, and Maya Angelou—
these are examples of people who found their "there." And we all felt it
when they found it. They are world-shaking personalities, but so are we
if we are "there." You say, "I don't feel like a hero or a world shaker." Well,
they probably didn't either. I remember when Martin Luther King, Jr.,
was alive. He wasn't being treated like a hero. There were no streets
named after him then. He had no national holiday in honor of his birth-
day. He was extremely controversial. The press accused him of being a
communist. But he was as much a hero then as he is now. He was living
in his "there." I only hope that there was someone around to tell him,
"You are there." If no one told him, he died not knowing that he was
"there." And so would you if it weren't for this message. Don't let the
controversial response of your Critics rob you of the reality of your destiny. You have to know it, taste it, and fulfill it. These people have little
in common outwardly, but each of them drew the world into their
"there" experience.

The challenge is to live in such a way that you wake up not only the
world but yourself to the totality of your calling. When you find it, it is
like the rich, exotic nectar of gratification warming and wetting the soul
with the juice of life itself. The quest is over; the nagging fear of failure
loses its grip. Suddenly, you will survive all obstacles, and problems are

just rude interruptions between the dance you are having with your soul. If you lose it or move away from it, bells start to ring. Alarms begin to sound within your heart. If you do not get back on course, your soul begins to ache and life itself begins to wither.

WISH YOU WERE HERE

When a person has escaped his arena, his destiny, or his purpose, his soul almost seems to weep. If you think about it, you will realize that you have seen it before—the weeping soul can be seen in sad eyes and dismal expressions. It is written on the face of many alcoholics. These are people who seek solace in the bottom-end of a bottle because they are mourning the loss of a place called "there." If you sit with them, they will tell you, "I was almost there," or I used to be "there." "What happened?" they lament. Like the homebound dreamer who receives postcards from veteran travelers that read, "Wish you were here," these sad pilgrims end up regretting the fact that they never visited the exotic islands of adventure themselves.

It is a sad reality to hear the bell start to ring and you have not found your "there." It causes couples to fight. Each one is blaming the other one for delaying them from their "there." In fact, the best love is shared between two people who are content to allow each other to maximize their time upon the earth and reach their "there." We generally love anyone who will help us or in any way encourage us to get "there." *You believed in me and I love you. You encouraged me to get there, and I will never forget you.* This is the pillow talk of grateful people who found a coach in the arms of their partners in destiny. There is no competition when there is mutual completion.

Unfortunately, there are relationships that cause the soul to twist and grimace in pain. Like an abused child, the soul withers, and finally somewhere alone in a room or driving down the road we hear the deep, gut-wrenching wailing of an anguished soul. The soul cries when our purpose is aborted, our destiny compromised, or our future detoured. I must warn you: If you are going to get "there," be careful to whom you join yourself. This road is so narrow and at times difficult. Don't let someone deter you, don't let someone push you off your path. It is difficult enough to get "there" without tying your wrist to a person who will cramp and hinder you. Remember, it is better to go lonely than not to go at all.

SOUL ACHES

When you are off your path, your soul will ache. It is not like a toothache, a backache, or a stomachache. You feel this pain in the deepest part of your essence. There is no medication that will correct it. The only thing that will ease an aching soul is repentance. That word simply means to turn around and go the other way.

Like all pain, a soul ache is a warning that something is wrong. The pain is an alarm that buzzes and screams when you have chosen a path that alters your course. It indicates that you have stepped out of your destiny and are lost.

I will tell you, sometimes my soul just breaks down and cries. Sometimes my life choices cramp my soul, and I know that this thing that I am doing is not for me. As bad as the pain may be, it is better to fix the problem and relieve the pain now than it is to lose the time, forfeit the race, and then hear the bell ring and not be "there." You see, some things that we try to do just don't fit the course of a God-given purpose. Then the soul aches like your feet in shoes that looked good in the window but just don't fit. You have to know when something doesn't fit.

Soul aches can be your compass. In my city, and likely in yours, there are several ways to get to the same place. I can take any one that I want and still get there. So it is with life. There are many ways that you can go to get to the same place. The path you take is your own choice. God is silent when you choose any of them, as it matters not which one you take as along as the destination is still the same. What you don't want to do is choose a path that takes you off course. But when you do make a choice that doesn't fit your life plan, God will let you know. Your soul will start to ache. It means that you are on the wrong road to get to the right end. When that happens, you have to say to whom or whatever it is that is making your soul ache, "No, this doesn't work for me. This shoe is not cut for my foot."

Why art thou cast down, O my soul? And why art thou disquieted within me?
(Psalm 42:11, KJV)

It is wise to occasionally take the time to reflect on where you are and to assess where you are going. But most of all, ask yourself how you are doing. You are probably the only person who will know how you are feeling and really stick around to hear the answer. So many have lost their passion and are living with a disturbed soul, which causes much internal pain. For many, it's a condition that causes restlessness, discontentment, and irritability. Others just become numb and indifferent about life, its pains or its pleasures. They lose the spark, their will to try to find "there." They often feel so lost in the dark wood, where all the trees, rocks, and landmarks look the same, that they can no longer sense their soul's compass. They cannot see the North Star because the branches are in the way.

Don't let life leave you numb and lost in the forest of indifference. It will if you let it. I shudder at all the things that threaten to leave you with soul paralysis. I have met people whose soul died on the journey, and they wandered the rest of their life with no compass. They wandered around being manipulated by others. They did so because they did not know how to reactivate the sensations in the soul.

The answer is this: Always, no matter how dark the day, live on, no matter how sad the circumstances, laugh on, and most of all, my friend, no matter how winding the journey, always go on. We will all have pleasure and pain, sunshine and rain; we will all laugh ourselves to tears one day and cry ourselves to sleep the next. These are the processes of the soul. I would rather have either than to be left numb and indifferent. The pleasure or pain of the soul is an indication that whatever is wrong can be repaired. It is proof that I am still alive: Tingling twitching, aching, swelling feelings connote life. I have made mistakes, confused signals, made bad choices, followed poor maps, made U-turns, but still, I am alive, and as long as I am alive there is time to benefit even from mistakes and dead-end detours.

If you have lost your way, pull over to the side of the road and ask for directions. God has the power to provide arrows pointing us back to our proper route. As the Psalmist tells us, "He restoreth my soul. . . ." (Psalm 23:3, KJV). If you are not sure that your decisions are lining up with your destiny, then listen within to the voice of God. He will speak in your soul, and He will restore it.

WHAT ARE YOU DOING HERE?

And after the fire came a gentle whisper. When Elijah heard it, he pulled his cloak over his face and went out and stood at the mouth of the cave. Then a voice said to him, "What are you doing here, Elijah?" (1 Kings 19:12–13, NIV)

The African slave women went way into the fields to groan beneath the load of a life that seemed out of control. Their bodies ached, their heads hung low, but they endured the pain. In the midst of their agony, they had slipped away. If you are ever going to hear your soul, you had better move away from the crowd. No one can hear their soul in a subway surrounded by noise and confusion. The old slaves headed for the woods, with their plain, ragged dresses swaying in the winds, and began to sing. Perhaps it was a song I heard as a child: "I went in the valley but I didn't go to stay. My soul got happy and I stayed all day." Yes, my soul has the power to "get happy" even when my back aches.

The survival instinct within us is a powerful tool. It enables us to endure unbearable things as long as we escape long enough to express that where we are is not where we are going. This confession is actually called hope. If we lose it, we have no strength for waking in the morning, no strength to fight for change, no power to endure. If you, like Elijah, find yourself in a cave of depression or fear, you must ask yourself a question: "What are you doing here?" If you find yourself involved in mediocrity when you were created to pursue higher exploits, ask yourself: "What are you doing here?" If your "here" is not your "there," you must begin to arise.

You must begin to compare your "here" with your "there." If you are not "there," and you are only "here," the other question that must be asked is this: "Is this 'here' a place on the way to 'there'?" If so, relax—it will take time, but you know you will get there. But if "here" is a cave of fear built on a decision to give in to the baser side of your fears or inhibitions, you must get up now. God asked Elijah, "What are you doing here?" because He knew that he was not created to be "here" when he could be "there."

No one can confront your "here" but you. You can't compare yourself with others because their purpose and yours may be two totally different things all together. Elijah had to find some place where he could get away from the screaming voices of fear and confusion and assess where he was. The "still, small voice" of God is the best map to truth. It is amazing that a God who uttered His voice and the earth melted can speak to those He loves in a hush so sweet that we must rise and come into his presence to better assess where we are and how to best regain our lost steps.

> *God is in the midst of her, she shall not be moved; God shall help her, just at the break of dawn. The nations raged, the kingdoms were moved; He uttered His voice, the earth melted. The LORD of hosts is with us; the God of Jacob is our refuge. Selah. Come, behold the work of the LORD, who has made desolations in the earth. He makes wars cease to the end of the earth; He breaks the bow and cuts the spear in two; He burns the chariot in the fire. Be still, and know that I am God; I will be exalted among the nations, I will be exalted in the earth! (Psalm 46:5–10, NKJV)*

Yes, he concludes with "be still and know." That is what we must do if we are going to get "there": We must be still and know that He is God. Yes, He is God even over mishaps and misfortunes. He is God over lost time. He is God over poor decisions. If you will listen and trust Him, He will lead you "there."

THE SUNDAY DRIVE

When I was a child, we used to get in the car and take a Sunday drive. We had all five of us in the car: my mom and dad, my sister and brother, and I. We would pack a lunch and hit the road. We did not know where we were headed. We just drove leisurely for hours looking at the scenery that God had provided for the poor, who had no other form of entertainment, no money for plays, no mentality for museums, and no opportunity for invitations to the social events of the day. We were just a carload of the then-called "colored people" driving a 1957 red and white rust-bucket of an automobile down the road into the thoroughfare, headed for nowhere, driving slowly and respectfully and sometimes a little fearfully depending on the neighborhood.

There were no appointments, no destinations, and no goals, just travel. That was the climate of the times. But just a few years later, we would move from Sunday leisure drives into the fast lane of life and enter the hustle almost as if my parents had heard the starting gun of a race go off. I guess they did. It was the signal of an age coming, and they had no real security. It was almost as if, while driving leisurely, someone had asked my dad, "What are you doing here? Have you no destination in mind?" I do not think that my father lacked ambition. He later owned a business of fifty-plus employees at a time when business owners didn't come in our color.

I believe that what made the Sunday drive pace last for so long was my dad's feeling that he was enslaved and trapped in a society that left few options. But when we trust God, we cannot allow the times to dictate the pace we take. We must be trendsetters and not march to the rhythm of the band. As we move forward, it is important that people of all classes and cultures do not spend their whole life on a Sunday stroll. The stroll is nice for a moment of repose, but if you are going to get to your place in life, you can't stay in the cave like Elijah. Nor can you take your family on a ten-year Sunday drive. Rest when you need, vacation when you will, but when all of that is done, put the pedal to the metal and drive.

I watched life from the backseat of a car then. I was a little boy watching the car mosey down the road and wondering where in the world were we going? Where were our people going? Where was I going? So many questions that I didn't know how or who to ask. I knew by looking into his eyes that my father wanted more than a Sunday drive out of life. I knew that he wanted more than an old raggedy car filled with poorly dressed children and a wife in a mail-order dress. He finally got his break too. He made great strides. Yes, the old man finally got the car in the fast lane and started moving. He built his company, built a new house complete with a patio (at a time when a patio was a suburban dream that only a few had attained), he got his dishwasher and all the now normal things that were luxuries at that time.

Later in life, I can still see him crossing his thin and frail legs that had just started to succumb to disease. He scratched his head with his thin fingers and looked out the patio door. I never knew what he was staring at. I just quietly watched, taking mental notes in the recesses of my mind. My father expired a few years after that. The doctors were beating on his chest trying to revive a failed heart that wore out after a long illness and renal failure, which ended his life at forty-eight.

As they lowered his body into the red Mississippi clay I think I finally figured out what my father was looking at every day as he sat on the patio. And for the first time in my life, I heard a small voice within myself. Maybe it was the voice that ignited him. Maybe it was my job to finish what he started. I do not know. All I know is that I walked slowly back to those shiny black cars to make the journey back from the cemetery with a conviction that I would keep hope alive and not stop until I was "there." My father saw it as he sat on the patio, and at that moment I saw it too. Each of us can see it if we will listen to the still, small voice within.

My father didn't leave me much. He left me a watch and a ring. Those things didn't mean much to me because I don't think they meant much to him. The real legacy he left me was the gleam in his eyes that I saw in the reflection from the rearview mirror of the 1957 Chevy. He left me the impassioned look from a pained heart that said come hell or high water you must do more than I did and reach farther than I reached. Well, my father's eyes saw it, his hands reached, his foot slipped, and he was gone. I am not certain, but I'll tell you what I believe happened: The bell rang, he had made great strides, but the game was over and my father died when he was almost . . . "there."

The legacy of my father's awareness of the place called "there" is what often sustains me on my journey. When the hours are long, when the betrayals of others oppress my soul with anguish, when I momentarily lose sight of the destination and wonder where I am in my cave of fearful depression, then I recall that gleam in my daddy's eye, that place where I first caught a glimpse of "there." Once you glimpse it yourself, your soul will never be content unless you fix your destination clearly in sight and get yourself on the path to getting "there."

My friend, you must stop and look at where you are on your life's map. Don't tell me you're too busy or too far behind to ever catch up. Don't tell me that you're too afraid of failure to get on the path. The only way we can ever truly maximize our moments is to make sure we are on the way to "there." Once we catch the vision for the quest of our lifetime, then so many other pieces fall into place. The hard work, the fears, the obstacles, and challenges—they all become worthwhile because they are a means to an end. Cast off your past failures, mistakes, wrong turns, and dead-ends. Change your direction to make sure you are moving toward the calling that will allow you to find the deep soul satisfaction that comes from knowing that "there" is inside us as much as it is a destination outside of us. From here to "there," my friend, is really not that far. There is great joy in the journey in knowing you are moving in the direction that will maximize all you have been created to be. Press on!

Not that I have already obtained all this, or have already been made perfect, but I press on to take hold of that for which Christ Jesus took hold of me. Brothers, I do not consider myself yet to have taken hold of it. But one thing I do: Forgetting what is behind and straining toward what is ahead. (Philippians 3:12–13, NIV)

TEN

—⟆⟅—

COUNTING UP
THE COST

For which of you, intending to build a tower, does not sit down first and count the cost, whether he has enough to finish it? (Luke 14:28, NKJV)

If you are going to build effectively, you have to have a strategy. Unfortunately, most people just sit around until they are confronted with a choice and then make a decision. No bank would give you money to build a house that had no blueprint or cost estimate. Neither will God invest resources into the hands of a person who has no plan. There is much to be said for a life that has a plan. Even if the plan has to be embellished, altered, or corrected, still there is a life plan. Early assessment of the following issues will assist you in preparing a plan before you are confronted with a choice. Then you can make your decisions based on your plan rather than the influences of the moment.

YOUR PLAN = DIVINE PURPOSE

The first thing you must do is to make sure your plan fits within the divine purpose for your life. The plan is the method whereby the purpose is accomplished. We, as humans, have no right to control the purpose, but we can assist in the developing of the plan. When we consider the divine purpose that has been set for each of us who knows that we are not here by mistake, it helps us to work in harmony with that divine purpose.

Admiration, though a wonderful thing, has caused many people to lose focus on finding what their purpose is and instead adopt someone else's purpose. No matter how inspirational someone else may be, his or her purpose is not yours. It is important that you maintain the right to be uniquely your own person with a distinct purpose. Do you not realize that all of your ability, talents, and resources have been predetermined so you can accomplish your purpose? They are like a toolbox of equipment and accessories that are God-given for your use to attain what He has determined. In other words, you are built to do what He has called you to accomplish.

This information is paramount for those who have a tendency not to appreciate their unique construction. You were built with a specific purpose in mind. There is a reason you have the personality that you do. There is a reason that you have the needs and abilities that you have. That doesn't mean that there are not areas in you that require discipline and focus. But I want you to realize that much of what God has endowed you with is neither good nor bad. It is neutral and nebulous until you use it for good or bad. It is like money: It becomes good or bad depending upon how you spend it. The same money that purchased an illegal drug could have been used to feed the hungry. If you do not know your purpose, your tools will be abused rather than used.

There are no worthless people, just people who have been misfiled, misappropriated, misallocated, those who need to be reassigned to the purpose for which they were created. Lacking a purpose causes us to squander our days and accomplish nothing. It causes us to feel like we are wandering aimlessly. This wandering feeling has driven many to drink, some to drugs, and others to suicide. The absence of purpose can cause a person to feel lost though they are living in their own house. It can make a person feel estranged though their own family surrounds them. Is there something missing from your life? Could it be an unrealized dream or an unrecognized purpose? What causes the soul to feel ill and the human spirit to feel like it is wandering with the passing of too many days with too little purpose?

COLLABORATE WITH THE CREATOR

When we do not know our purpose, we wander around ineffectively even though we expend a lot of effort. We move our feet on the treadmill of life, but we fail to cover the miles of terrain that are required to move toward our goal. The failure to ascertain our purpose comes when we fail to consult and develop a spiritual base for our lives. It is when we consult God that He directs us into His divine purpose and we establish together a plan that is much like a prebuilding consultation among the architects, the contractors, and the owners.

Many people depend on God to do everything. While that sounds good, it really doesn't make sense. There are some things that humans have contributed to since the beginning of Creation. They named the animals, built the ark, and built God's own house, the Temple in Jerusalem. It is imperative that we, through collaboration, develop a feel for the plan. God in His grace allows us to contribute to the plan as long as it doesn't alter the purpose. It saves countless misunderstandings and wasted effort when communication exists between you and the Divine Architect.

Most of us never consult anyone; we just wake up in the morning and start hammering. The tragedy is that much of what we have then built has to be scrapped and redone. We marry people without looking at the plan. We make career choices without looking at the plan. These choices are often based on the finances, convenience, or some other peripheral issue. But the choice should rest solely on the purpose of God. Does this move take me closer or further from my life's goal and purpose? That is the question. If the answer is no, then why are you wasting days moving toward it?

ON WITH THE SHOW

It doesn't hurt to weigh friendships in the light of purpose. Be careful of old friends, especially when you have made massive life changes. There are some who are friends for a lifetime. But many times we choose friends based on old lifestyles. When we change, we are left trying to maintain old friendships, which require that we do an encore of an old show we do not want to perform anymore. Seldom will you find someone who can grow with you. When you do, it is wonderful. If you don't, move on. The choices are quite simple. Either you move on at the risk of separating from them, or you separate from your goal so that you can stay connected to them. Some of them seem jealous, when actually they are confused and intimidated. They connected with who you were, and now you have changed. They do not want to go where you are going, and they resent being driven into your life changes. And now they are giving you grief, either publicly or secretly. They are discontent over the prospect of having to grow with you. Remember that smiling faces do not always tell what the mind is thinking. Smiling faces may be blocking sacred spaces that you are called to explore.

I am not suggesting that your friends be chosen because of what they can do to assist you in accomplishing your purpose. They are not your source. God is your source, and you should rely upon Him and the talents that He gave you. But I would say that there are some relationships that not only do not assist you, they are, in fact, a liability that takes you away from your goal. When you meet people, ask yourself a question. Your question is not, "Can they go with me?" The question must be, "Can they grow with me?" No wonder our relationships do not last. We make permanent decisions about temporary needs. We never have the consultation meeting, and yet we add these relationships to our lives. It would be like using a low-grade lumber to build a mansion because it is cheaper and it looks the same as the expensive stuff. You don't look at the specs the architect designed for the building. Years pass and the house is falling apart. The inferior wood could not stand up against time, weather, and other forces of nature. You wonder what went wrong. You never had a preplanning meeting with the architect, you never looked at his plan.

BUILD WITH PURPOSE

For we are laborers together with God: ye are God's husbandry, ye are God's build-
ing. According to the grace of God which is given unto me, as a wise masterbuilder,
I have laid the foundation, and another buildeth thereon. But let every man take
heed how he buildeth thereupon. (1 Corinthians 3:9–10, KJV)

The ultimate purpose is the reason you have been given this time in the first place. If you do not know your purpose and you do not have your plan, you will waste your time. Most people fall into the cesspools of life because they have not known their purpose.

Counterproductive relationships and decisions, then, are those persons, places, and things that take you further away from your life's goals. Please note that we are often attracted to things that are counterproductive. But we must not choose by attraction, we must choose by direction. If it is not in the direction you want to end up in, why go there? Constantly looking at the purpose allows you to resist the temptation to plan anything that will not accomplish that purpose. We have to respect the purpose. That, within itself, is a form of worship as it acknowledges the masterbuilder of your life to be God and not you. It acknowledges God and not your past. The Bible says, "In all thy ways acknowledge him, and he shall direct thy paths" (Proverbs 3:6, KJV). If you want direction with the plan, then acknowledge His purpose.

If you will respect that principle, your mishaps will diminish. When you do have mishaps, they will not be debilitating because you have a purpose that you live by. By keeping God's purpose in mind, you will choose the right course of action that will assist you in righting the wrong choices, which all of us make from time to time. But keep the plan in alignment with the purpose as much as you can. It will stop you from having to waste so much time correcting and enduring mistakes.

SEIZE THE SEASON

The second thing you must consider when you count costs is: Where are you in the stages of life? Are you caught up in surviving the season, or can you maintain your course even through winter storms and summer heat? You must assess your current life stage if you are to know how to continue.

> *There is a time for everything, and a season for every activity under heaven.* (Ecclesiastes 3:1, NIV)

You may have wondered why some people are successful. It seems like they know exactly what to do. Well, that is not all there is to it. They also know when to do it. There is nothing as tragic as someone who doesn't recognize that they are doing the right thing at the wrong season. You are most effective when you are bringing forth fruit in your season. That is where the blessing occurs. You cannot do it whenever you want to do it. You have to do it in your season. What is a season? This word "season" is translated from the Hebrew word "zeman," which means an appointed time. An appointed time is an allotted time that has been predisposed to accomplish an act or an event. It is the fruit-bearing time. It is when all of the elements are conducive for accomplishment. It is the convergence of conditions to produce the best fruit: the weather, the maturity of the tree, the cross-pollination, the rain, the pruning. Each complements the other elements so that together they may fulfill the tree's function, to bear fruit. When the right season comes along, it almost seems to effortlessly produce what has been buried within the tree.

There is fruit that is buried within you. You can produce it effectively and powerfully, but only in your season. The four seasons of nature will be a good model for you to plan your marriage, career, family, and all other issues pertaining to life, because in all areas of life, you will have a spring, summer, autumn, and a winter. Know what season you are in. Know which is your fruit-bearing season and which is your fruit-gathering time. Then there will be a fruit-preserving time and, finally, you will survive in the winter off of what you grew in the spring, gathered in the summer, and preserved in the fall. Planning ahead according to the present season allows you to remain on course even when the conditions are not naturally conducive to your journey's fulfillment.

What season are you in? Do you know? You may be in different seasons depending on what area we are discussing. For example, you may be in the winter of raising your children, but you may have recently remarried and your intimate relationship may be in spring. Your career may be in summer. There are different rules for each season. You need to figure out what season you're in for each area of your life, and then act accordingly.

While the earth remaineth, seedtime and harvest, and cold and heat, and summer and winter, and day and night shall not cease. (Genesis 8:22, KJV)

THE INFANCY OF SPRING

Spring will always be your planning and growth years; it is the time of accomplishment. It is during this time that the sap you need to build is flowing to you and through you. You have the sap of patience, the sap of tenacity, the sap of perseverance; you need to launch a business, build a home, establish a marriage, raise your children, or whatever the purpose is that you have been assigned. Start it with gusto and establish it with definite strength, not passive indifference. You will waste this moment if you are docile.

Spring is the time of passion. It is during this season that you have the greatest passion to do the greatest things. You do not need to be enhanced, motivated, or encouraged to do naturally at this season what you may have to be induced to do in another season. This is the budding stage. The budding of love. The budding of your company. This is the budding of your child's development and character. Whatever it is you are developing is birthed but still infantile.

Spring is exciting and new. Like a new movie, it is your opening night. But remember, you are only new once. Spring is beautiful and forceful, but it will not last. Don't waste this time fussing. It is a time to work hard and fast. Tomorrow you will go from new and improved to normal and ordinary.

This stage requires care and grooming. Do not expect spring to possess maturity. It is unwise for you to become frustrated with things that have not existed long enough to be mature. Maturity takes time. Whatever you are doing in the spring has to be trained and disciplined to maturity. This is the youth of your seasons. Let no man despise your youth.

I am not merely speaking of an age but an era. You might be seventy years old, but you just started something that you have fresh passion for, and you are in your youth about that particular issue. It is springtime in your soul!

SUMMER'S STABILITY

Summer is the blazing hot era in which you maintain what you have birthed. The infancy is over. This is the time of stability. It is during this time that you stabilize what God has done in your life. Plan to stabilize what you have accomplished. Stability takes time. It will not be done easily. It is during this time that you "lengthen thy cords, and strengthen thy stakes" (Isaiah 54: 2, KJV). It is your breaking-forth time. This is the season when you have come into your own. You have some assurance and you feel comfortable. You have lost the nervous jitters of spring, and you have come into a level of consistency. You have earned a few stripes and carry a few bruises, but you are developing confidence. I don't mean arrogance, but a confidence that comes when you have been around for a while.

Your life has been established and identified, labeled and classified. It is during this stage that you perfect what spring has produced. The summer with its glaring sun is the time of increase. It is during this time that you see the increase of the pure little thing you saw sprout in spring. Summer, then, is the time of multiplicity. Now notice this: Whatever you experienced in its infancy in Spring, whether it is good or bad, will multiply in this season. New blessings probably, new troubles definitely. It goes with the turf. I always say new levels bring new devils. Expect the growth of both the positive and the negative. This is the time when much is being given to you. This is also the time when much will be required of you. If it's a child, you have less work in dressing the child;

186/ T. D. JAKES

they can do that now. But now they have more attitudes and personality struggles. If it is a company, you have a greater profit margin, but now you have tax issues, employee problems, legal issues, and competitive jealousy. No one seemed jealous of you before because you were struggling. Jealousy may be your first sign of summer. If you are applying this to marriage, this is the time when you are settling into comfortable roles. You now have a nicer place to stay. You have acquired some things, perhaps a career or a baby. You have some things to show for your investment together. But more effort is required to maintain passion. You are still in love, but at this stage, recognize that you are married to a human being. The proverbial "honeymoon" is over, and you are starting to see what his mother tried to tell you. Perhaps you do not regret your decision, but you better realize that commitment to marriage is necessary or the maintenance goes down. The spring buds of love dimmed your vision and hindered you from seeing that the wonderful person you married may not be as easy to live with as you thought when you repeated those vows that are said quickly but lived slowly. But all of that is part of summer, and you will have it: the strengths of and weaknesses from developing stability.

MATURITY IN AUTUMN

It is in this stage that you are settled. You have produced your fruit. You have matured in many areas, and you know now what to expect and also how to cope with what you have to work with. You have adjusted your expectations and have benefited from the experiences: the knocks and bruises of life.

This is the time of calmness. You are not easily rattled by anything. You have been there and done that. You are prepared for the changes of life. It is at this stage that you reap the benefits of longevity. You do not have the blazed passion of youth, but you have the stately calm of the seasoned veteran. If you are wise, you are now working smarter and not harder. You know now what you wish you had known then. You are using your head because you have been around long enough to know a few things.

It is at this stage that you also realize more acutely that all that you have gathered will be passed on to someone or something. You suddenly become cognizant of the fact that success is not complete without a successor. It is this mid-life issue that is the real crisis. Whether it is the mid-life of a person or a company, you suddenly realize that the day-to-day issues that confront you are not of great concern. Now you have to focus on preparing for the changing of seasons. You realize that what was once popular will not be tomorrow. The methods of doing business are changing. The child has turned into a man. The marriage has changed from passion to partnership. The clock is ticking and you look up from budding in spring and building in summer and assess not just what you have but where you are as a person.

The sap is going down, the passion is ebbing, and the leaves are turning. This is the time of changing. The job doesn't change, the season does. With those changes come the final burst of colorful leaves. The company is as diverse as a peacock, but also less malleable and more regimented. The marriage is filled with portfolios, pictures, and momentos, but health issues have started to come into play. You savor the moments but realize that your life has peaked in many arenas. It is time to transition and prepare for the upcoming winter; how you have stocked your storehouse will inevitably affect your quality of life in the years to come.

People often blow it right here and lose all they have attained. They fail to plan for the winter. They fail to name a successor. Autumn is winter's last warning. Draw up a check list while you still have the strength to make amendments and corrections. Make a retirement check. An insurance check. An estate-planning check. A downsizing-need check. You need to be prepared to enter the next season.

WINTER'S RIGIDITY

This is the stage that defies flexibility. It is the stage when ideas have become so formalized that tradition has become a focal point. It is in the winter that the traditions are maintained with passion because that is all that is familiar. All else is giving way to change and rebirth as life prepares for the next generation of people, of companies, of ideas.

There are at this level new trends, doctrines, ideas and concepts, yet the winter stage does not lend itself to the elasticity of change. Nor should it. There is nothing worse than a winter stage trying to pass itself off as a spring. It is as ridiculous as an old lady in hot pants. Or an old man cruising down the boulevard in biker shorts

This is the time that you assess your accomplishments, enjoy your assets, pass on your counsel, and take your bows. You have fought the good fight, kept the faith, and finished the course. This means that you have fulfilled your purpose, and that is what success is all about. The only time winter is unwelcome is when it comes before completion. Whatever you are going to do and be, do it before winter.

Do thy diligence to come before winter . . . (2 Timothy 4:21, KJV)

We must seize the day before night comes creeping over the hill and catches us with our work undone. Night cometh, my friend. It is coming, and that is not a bad thing. The only bad thing is that it often catches us still wrestling with the decisions and issues that were not reconciled in the right season before the first snowfall freezes our productivity and limits our opportunities.

I am reminded of Jacob. In the winter of their lives, all great men do the same thing: They give away what they have gathered; they share their wisdom and resources because they suddenly realize that none of the trophies goes home with you. Jacob was no different. When he was old, he called his sons around his bed. He addressed Benjamin, his son whose loins held unborn kings, spoke to him about potential and greatness, and left a word about seasons that has inspired me throughout my life.

> *Benjamin is a ravenous wolf; in the morning he shall devour the prey, and at night he shall divide the spoil.* (Genesis 49:27, NKJV)

From his winter bed, as life ebbed from his body and death waited patiently in the corner, Jacob taught his son that the morning, the youth of a thing, is the time when you devour the prey in your life. You do all of your attacking when it is early. It is in your youthful passion that you conquer your foes. It is then that you are ravenous as a wolf. It is in the youth of a thing that your appetites are keen and your passions insatiable. That is the power you use to devour your opposition.

He then tells Benjamin that in the night you must divide the spoils. If you are going to enjoy life, you must know when to devour the prey and when to divide the spoils. He tells his son to do the right thing in the right season. Most people make the mistake of trying to divide the spoils too soon, leading to bankruptcy and defeat. Others try to devour the prey too late, leading to the death of the dream and the dreamer. *It is doing the right thing at the right time that determines success.* When Jacob had taught that final lesson to his sons, he folded his legs in the bed, kissed his children goodbye, and went to the land of his fathers; and so will we all.

CHOICES AND CHANCES

The third principle in this process of assessing the costs of our dreams before we continue on our journey is this: We must develop choices and chances. Each day is God's gift to you. What you do with it is your gift to Him. We are weighted down with the responsibility of choice. Why doesn't anyone tell us that we have chances to change the day by the choices we make? We are left blindly stumbling around. We grope for hope in dark days without the bright light of decision shining on life's issues. We stumble unaided by the strong arm of choices and chances to alter life's dark places. It took me half of my life to discover the great power of choices and chances.

We drape our lack of courage in the frayed tapestry of fate. The piercing rays of truth still leak through the loosely woven excuses that give alibis to the guilty heart, which failed to alter circumstances. We then dismiss our responsibility like a cheap attempt at religious absolution, living in denial that things could have been better had we taken action sooner. The worst part of it is that many foolishly charge God and hold Him liable for things they could have changed.

God gives to us a chance. He graces us with opportunities, each day being a gift to be unwrapped and enjoyed. We must seize each moment as an adventure. If we are aware of the precious potential of each new day, our hearts will be penetrated with the urgency to make each moment count toward eternity. Life's chances come like light, 186,000 miles an hour, and pass us before we can understand from whence they come or where they go. It is what the Bible calls the breaking of day. Day breaks, night ends, and you are afforded one more chance to right wrongs, overcome obstacles, and embrace unrealized potentials.

Catch the light like a baseball player catches a fast ball. Get your mitt and get ready to catch your chance. It will not wait. It will come. If you are not there, it will pass. Whatever happens thereafter, always remember that you had a chance. You had a chance not to marry her. You had a chance to answer that knock at the door. You had a chance to say, "I want out." But one thing is sure: You had the chances, and the choices are yours. So you must say every day, "I'll take my chances, activate my choices, go through my changes, and make my decisions." And when the day is done, you will say to yourself, "It was my life and I played it to the fullest."

Does destiny play a part? You bet it does. The issue is quite simple. Are you living out your destiny? Have you satisfied the craving of your soul and reached your predetermined destination? Or are you wasting time, spending too much time here rather than "there"? No matter what else you attain, no matter what else you aspire to accomplish, if you fail to grasp what your real purpose is and pursue it, then death is tragic and life is sad. The ultimate success is accomplished when we get to the end of all the building and struggling of life and find that the house we built looks like the design we had been given. If we build anything else, we may gain the praises of men, but it will cost us the inner peace and fulfillment that only comes when we have done what we were placed here to do. We want to hear our Master say, "Well done, thy good and faithful servant" (Matthew 25:23, NKJV). We want to count up the cost of fulfilling our dreams in order that we may pay as we go along for a prize beyond compare.

ELEVEN

DRIVING BLIND

When we start to discuss self-perception, I know that many will respond by saying, "I don't need to go there. I know who I am." They will claim an exception from suffering low self-esteem. Well, I salute you. But let's enter into the subject for just a moment or two. You see, it is possible to know who you are and yet not be conscious of where you are. Self-perception embraces self-esteem, but it also includes self-monitoring: knowing where you are at all times compared to where you are going. It is vital to do this from time to time so that you can make sure you're on the right track for fulfilling your purpose and achieving success.

Now, although feeling good about oneself is the essential fuel to drive you to succeed, some affirm themselves to the point that they seem engrossed in a private love affair with themselves. Self-centered, self-congratulatory, self-absorbed, their entire lives are a celebration of the self, and no one else is invited to the party.

On the other end of the spectrum are those who are their own worst enemy. They are never good enough, smart enough, or pretty enough. They are just never enough in their own eyes. Failures are magnified and accomplishments dismissed as undeserved luck. These poor souls never taste the sweet fruit of success, for their low self-esteem is a bitter bile that coats their mouths and robs them of pleasure.

For most of us, hopefully by the time we reach the age of maturity we have gained the wisdom and self-assurance to balance the delicate scale of self-esteem: neither too vain nor self-punishing. We learn to develop a healthy pride for our accomplishments and a humble respect for the talents we have been gifted with.

Unfortunately, once self-esteem is no longer an issue, we tend to forget about it, putting it on the back burner of our life, because we have too many other things to think about. Most people are so busy being productive that they tend to neglect themselves and seldom dignify themselves with the importance that they need. But when you do not take time to appreciate yourself, the pot will boil over, the contents will scorch you, and you will be left with a burned-out mess. Then you are so vulnerable to anyone who does offer you the slightest drop of praise that you become susceptible to moral failure that is born out of thirst. Take time to refresh yourself and appreciate yourself. And then before you become too engrossed with the ecstasy, go back to work!

PERILOUS MOBILITY

Many successful people seldom celebrate what they have accomplished or where they are in life due to the "blind spot." A blind spot, every driver soon learns, is that place when the approaching object is so close that he or she cannot see it even in the mirror. All those around him may see it, but it is hidden from his view. His position has affected his perception. If you are going to maintain mobility, perception is vital. Without proper perception, you are in a perilous situation.

The life traveler is like a driver who can see through the windshield. Hence, she can discern the future. She has a clear view straight ahead and her eyes are fixed on the distant horizon. It is excellent to be a visionary, but sometimes looking ahead can prevent people from living in the present. The proverbial carrot is always in front of them. They are "someday" people. They have gone from delayed gratification, which can be healthy, to denied gratification, which can be debilitating. Every happiness is postponed, every celebration put off, waiting on some futuristic goal to be attained. These people have never had a reckoning day. Delayed has become denied, and they are the ones causing the denial.

The life traveler can also look through the rearview mirror and see her past. She can reminisce over the many obstacles she had to overcome to get to the place where she is now. She can look behind and watch as she moves beyond her limitations and leaves them in the dust. But, some people could get on with their lives if they didn't live in the rearview mirror. Everything that they think about themselves comes from their incessant need to keep looking back. The past seems more familiar than the present or the future. They are stuck in a stage of reverse reasoning. They think more about what has happened than they do about what will happen. Their eyes are fixed to the rear view of life, and sooner or later they are going to crash.

Yes, if you are going to drive successfully you must look straight ahead and know where you are going. You must use your rearview mirror from time to time to reassess the obstacles you have passed and make sure they aren't threatening you anymore. But the best of drivers constantly gauges their present situation: where they are, how fast they are going, how much gas they've got left in the tank. They keep their hands on the wheel, their eyes constantly moving, and they are always alert to the fact that there is a blind spot they need to be cautious of.

A good driver is always cautious and alert. If you are not alert, you are a liability to all who ride with you through life. No one wants to ride with a distracted driver. You must be focused and deliberate. I can assure you that I have never met anyone who has succeeded by mistake. Succeeding at anything requires deliberation and intentional effort and aim. I know it is possible to go beyond your wildest dreams and to acquire more than you ever thought possible. Many of you will exceed your own expectations, especially once you stop limiting those expectations. But no one achieves or accomplishes prolonged success accidentally.

OUT OF SIGHT

You must always be alert to your blind spot, but that's tricky because you cannot see it. Many have crashed because of the blind spot, that small area whereby your perception is impaired by your position and you have trouble seeing what's right upon you. Our blind spots are our weaknesses, areas in our lives that prevent us from seeing and being in the present. Our blind spots prevent us from accurately assessing our current situation. We all have them. Whether you are driving a rust-bucket or a Rolls, there will always exist that one common denominator: the "blind spot."

I am reminded of my mother in the last years of her life. When Mother was in her thirties, she collected some lovely china pieces that she kept in her curio cabinet. The china was to be admired and appreciated. We hardly ever used these exotic-looking, precious dishes; they were reserved for some special occasions. Some of the china was still kept in its original boxes. Forty-some years had passed, and she still had dishes that she was saving for company. I often told her, "Mom, if the company hasn't come by now, then they aren't coming. Break out the china and eat on it yourself. You bought it, you earned it, and someday is today." It is appreciating and using these little momentos that help us know that we have arrived. That makes perfect sense, doesn't it? But it was hard for her to see. Do not laugh at her; I bet you have "somedays" yourself. A vacation you can't afford to take yet; a pedicure that you won't get done; teeth you won't repair. Things that you put on hold for no good reason other than the fact that you are still struggling with the past or living in denial with your eyes on the future.

For my mother, it was the former. You see, my mom and some of her siblings went through the Great Depression of the 1930s. The depression has been over for decades, but they are still afraid that it will come back again. If it does, they will say, "We know how to survive—we can make it." Well, that made more sense when they were younger and struggling to regain their economic footing. But they made it, retired from their jobs, and no one ever told them that they were "there." They were very intelligent, resourceful people, but they, like all of us, had a "blind spot."

What I am trying to get you to see is the danger of being "there" and not knowing it. All too often we do not recognize where we are. We have a blind spot.

One has to wonder: Did Martin Luther King, Jr., know in his lifetime the magnitude of his contribution? Did he know that one day every major city in this nation would have a memorial, a highway, or a facility named after him? Probably not, because in his lifetime, he was not referred to as a hero. They referred to him as a rebel. They beat him and turned hoses on him and, though today he is considered a civil rights hero, he probably didn't feel like one. His greatness existed before he died, but it was probably in his "blind spot."

I watched in amazement as newscasters reported that Princess Diana had met her untimely death. It was a sad occasion all over the world. People traveled from across the globe just to drop lovely roses in front of the regal gates of Buckingham Palace. As far as the eye could see, mourners and spectators alike silently and somberly gathered and stood for hours to express the magnitude of their grief. Their sorrow went beyond the loss of a princess—it encompassed the loss of a stately grace that was once revered and respected by all people. Diana represented what little girls once held sacred. She had exploded onto our television sets as the bride of the century. She, with lace-clad hands and silky, smooth, satiny-soft trains of buoyancy, had sashayed across the camera lens as a modern-day testimony to a regal fairy tale come true. Every little girl from every culture had dreamed it was her wedding day.

We watched as the millions of dollars spent on the wedding failed to keep Diana and her Prince together. They tired to maintain the romantic illusion, but allegations of infidelity and misery invaded the locked chambers of their privacy, and the dream wedding slowly turned into a nightmare. We were there as the Princess redefined her goals, survived her tragedies, realigned her mission, and became known as a great humanitarian. We saw her fame turn to harassment and abuse as the paparazzi made her life miserable, treating her like a rare animal to be put on public display.

And now here we were as the sad remains of a dream awakened to a horrifying reality. Reporters who had nearly assaulted her now fought back tears and dropped their voices into a sad monotone pitch. They sighed and spoke softly as they televised tear-jerking pictures of her children, her wedding, and anything else they could find to highlight their need for a fresh glimpse of a modern tragedy. Her pictures faded on some stations; they were black and white on others to suggest death. She was paraded in slow motion to sad music and falling leaves. The world from Japan to New York cried; the world was pained by the loss of a great giver of beauty and life.

I, too, sat there watching with the rest of the grieving world, tasting my own flavor of pain. Not the personal blinding pain that I am sure her sons must have felt, not the conflict of emotions that I am sure her now-estranged husband must have felt. But I felt for Diana. No, I did not know her, but I had known a hundred Dianas before her. Lovely women whose greatness was never heralded when they could have heard it. I mourned the fact that she would have been so blessed to see her impact

on the world. Yes, I know she was famous, but now she was immortal-
ized as an international heroine. She was featured and honored in the papers and magazines that once had painted her as a shallow socialite. All
of that is the way the machine works and the world turns. But, I wondered: Did she know in life what was now realized in death? I asked myself, "Did she know she was 'there'?"

Poor Diana, I thought. She would have loved to have seen this display
of love. I hoped silently that someone had given her a fitting tribute
while she was still alive to hear it. Most of us miss the glory while we create the story. We seldom read our own print, and when we do, it is the
negative voice of criticism that screams the loudest over all else.

*"The days are coming," declares the LORD, "when the reaper will be overtaken by
the plowman and the planter by the one treading grapes. New wine will drip from
the mountains and flow from all the hills." (Amos 9:13, NIV)*

When things begin to break loose, it happens so quickly that you
seldom have a chance to adjust your perception and access where you
are. The planter will have just planted grape seeds that are ready to be
treaded into wine. That is pretty fast. All the while in this rapid stage of
life, you have a tendency not to see where you are.

In all reality, you could be "there" and not know it. You may have accomplished your goal and been so driven that you have failed to recognize where you are. It is sad to work all of your life to get to a place and
not really recognize your destination when you get there. Most people
reach their goals and do not enjoy the goals that they reach. They do not
always recognize where they are because they are looking in the rearview
mirror, wrestling with how hard it was to get there. They are still having an affair with past pains and traumas. Or they are looking through
the windshield at what is ahead, not accessing or appreciating what is
there right now.

Before she passed away, I was speaking with my mom one day. She was teasing me about being so busy. I dropped my head like the little boy that she brings out in me and said, "I am where you were in your forties. Don't you remember when you were working with one hand, raising us with the other, rushing to meetings, answering the phone, resolving conflicts, ironing out situations, and trying to squeeze in a bath before Saturday?" She laughed and said, "Yes, I do." She said it seemed like a blur. She patted me with her wrinkled hands and looked at me through her cataracts and said, "Son, enjoy it. It goes by so quickly." I knew she was trying to tell me that I was missing the best years of my life by focusing only on the stress of my life. I was living in the "blind spot."

THE SIDEVIEW MIRROR

Now, anyone who is a driver may be thinking, "All you need to do is use your sideview mirror to avoid disaster because of your blind spot." The mirror does assist you in perceiving what you are not positioned to determine. The only problem with this tool of perception is that you are dealing with two moving objects. You are trying to evaluate the distance of something that is moving while you are moving yourself. Because of this, you cannot accurately assess how near something is to you. There is a message imprinted on the base of the side mirror that reads "Approaching Objects May Be Closer Than They Appear." Here lies the vulnerability of self-analysis. If you were not in the car, you could readily tell how close you were to your approaching success. But from your position, you cannot determine it. Again, think of it: Approaching objects may be closer than they appear.

For this reason, we must be ever vigilant on our journeys, staying alert and cautious, driving ahead steadily and determinedly, but not recklessly. We may not be able to see our blind spot, but we can be as pre-pared for it as we can be when it comes.

Also, I must tell you that the blind spot does not only hide negative things. No, blessings can be hidden there too. Blessings may be closer than they appear.

> *And it shall come to pass, if thou shalt hearken diligently unto the voice of the* LORD *thy God, to observe and to do all his commandments which I command thee this day, that the* LORD *thy God will set thee on high above all nations of the earth: And all these blessings shall come on thee, and overtake thee, if thou shalt hear-ken unto the voice of the* LORD *thy God. (Deuteronomy 28:1–2, KJV)*

When God is involved, He causes the blessings to overtake you. These blessings seem to come out of nowhere. You will not just receive what you are seeking. There are some things that will find you and overtake you. Most people of faith and tenacity will admit that there are some un-explained blessings and benefits that just occurred in their lives while they were laboring in pursuit.

Yes, it is important to have a goal. It is important to pursue with all diligence that which you are convinced is your "there-ness," but always leave room for the approaching blessing that just comes and overtakes you while you are driving along the highway of life.

DRIVING LESSONS

My friend, we must all become good drivers. From time to time, we should glance in the rearview mirror to see what is in our past. We want to avoid being overtaken by something in our past that might sneak up on us unawares. We must look in the sideview mirror and assess what is

202 / T. D. JAKES

next to us right now. What is alongside us? We must cover our blind spots by being aware of them and by seeking outside perspective on our journey and the obstacles that might attempt to run us off the road. Then we must keep our eyes looking ahead through the windshield to see where we are headed.

Are you enjoying the journey as you head toward your destination? Or are you so consumed with the past that you tailgate someone and crash into their bumper? Have you stopped on the shoulder to take in a panoramic view or to wait out a thunderstorm? Those moments are necessary breaks, but we must press on and continue our journey. Get back in your car and start the engine and move toward the place called "there." Keep your eyes on the scenery around you, consult a map when necessary, and thereby maximize the process of attaining your promised land, the ultimate destination of this journey called life.

————◆————

TWELVE

WE'RE NOT IN KANSAS ANYMORE

The Wizard of Oz has been hailed as America's favorite movie and is based on a story by L. Frank Baum. It premiered in play form at the Majestic Theatre in New York on January 20, 1939. Since its debut almost one hundred years ago, it has been a treasured favorite of people everywhere. Many of them will always remember seeing it as I did, perched on the tired lap of my overworked, underpaid father, who was trying to spend a moment of quality time with his children many years ago.

While my mother was busy throwing hash in her kitchen and washing dishes in a pan fitted into the chipped sink, I was watching the little girl named Dorothy. Dorothy, who starts out in Kansas, finds herself hurled away from her humble home into the air and ultimately into a foreign, fanciful world. She spends the entire movie trying to find the wizard so he can send her home.

You may ask what *The Wizard of Oz* has to do with maximizing the moment. Well, if you are motivated to maximize this moment we call life, sooner or later you will find yourself hurled up into a windstorm of change and maneuvered into a new environment, which seems almost extraterrestrial compared to the Kansas where you were raised. But unlike

204 / T. D. JAKES

Dorothy, we will not be in search of the wizard. Rather, we will be pushing forward to see what we can be and do. That desire will never be attained if we lie facedown in the bed of mediocrity and surround ourselves with familiar faces and stop short of exploring new dimensions of life.

I want to challenge you, as I have been challenged over and over again, to spread your wings and fly into the wind of a society beyond your dreams and far into your fears. It is there, in a place that I will call Oz, that we discover the greatest education and the best opportunity to become all that destiny has in store for us. You must push your borders beyond Kansas.

I am not at all suggesting that you forget from where you came, but I am declaring that when you remember from where you came, it ought to be at a safe distance away from it. Admittedly, those persons, places, and things of your past may be the foundation on which your life is erected, but please, extend yourself so that you can experience a taste of the intoxicating variety of life and thereby be escorted into the limitless potentials that occur when we move forward into the land of dreams, desires, and potentials.

SYNCHRONIZED SWIMMING

In order to maximize your moment, you will have to bury your fears of rejection and go beyond what you know into a world of limitless potential. You will have to allow new people and things into your life if you are going to grow and keep moving ahead. These new associations will be alien to you, and that may be intimidating at times, but you must do this to reach the next level in life.

If the blind lead the blind, they both fall into the ditch. This old adage suggests that it is imperative that we surround ourselves with people who complement us rather than duplicate us. We need to have access to people who see differently than we do and who can help us on our way. Yet, many of us find ourselves keeping company with, and being led by, people whose insight is no deeper than our own. In essence, the blind are leading the blind. While this tendency makes little sense, it is often the reality. You see, it is quite natural for us to commonly seek those who are similarly suited.

Recently, while on vacation in Nassau I spent hours watching schools of fish swimming together. Bright blue fish moved gracefully through the water, turning from one direction to the other in perfect unison. Another group danced through the water together, a colorful parade of yellow and red. It was beautiful to watch them move gracefully and systematically through the currents of water. It was like the elaborate dance numbers in those old Esther Williams water musicals: the beauty and uniformity of synchronized swimming. The Caribbean Sea was filled with various types of aquatic species. Although they shared the same waters, food, and oxygen, they didn't travel in schools with other types of fish. No, each stayed with its own kind

This tendency to surround oneself with the familiar is not limited to fish. Birds migrate in flocks. Wolves move in packs. Even we humans have a tendency to divide ourselves into groups of similar types. In some cases, the basis of the division is race. In others it is education. Still others divide into social spheres based on similar occupations. Humans have divided into every conceivable group. One need only ride through any city, talk to any realtor, to know that the wealthy areas are generally not shared by the impoverished. The middle class usually dwells within blocks of each other. We are like the fish swimming with company who laugh at the same things, vote the same party, and have the same ideas about life, love, and business.

When you surround yourself with people with whom you have so much in common, I suppose that there is a sense of safety that comes from knowing what is expected of you. But it is comparable to living your life in a small glass fishbowl. It is safe and self-contained, but it is also very small and confining. You feel protected, insulated from any contaminates, but you are denied any greater gift than the smug satisfaction that you are living in a very secure world.

The real opportunity to be enhanced comes when we are exposed to diversity. That diversity challenges narrow-mindedness and stimulates growth. God created us to be different and unique.

The sun has one kind of splendor, the moon another and the stars another; and star differs from star in splendor. (1 Corinthians 15:41, NIV)

The heavenly bodies all have their own type of beauty, but together they make the night sky a brilliant, breathtaking extravaganza. Likewise, we will shine even brighter if we are with people who are different from us. It is this kind of enhancement that ignited the foreign exchange programs that have become popular with many students around the world. These programs provide a chance for a student from one part of the world to taste the exotic influence of other people's cultures. A boy from Nebraska can visit Nepal and discover a broader canvass of human relationships, culture, and communication. A girl from India can come to Indiana and learn to reassess her perspective on wealth and poverty, sickness, and health.

INTEGRATION EXPECTATION

My purpose is not merely to discuss racial or cultural integration. My purpose is to encourage another type of integration—the integration that is necessary to enlarge your sphere of influence beyond what it is right now. If you are going to go to the next level in life, you must surround yourself with people who are there, even when you are not. You must overcome your fear of rejection. It is this fear that often intimidates people from going forward. You would be surprised how many people limit themselves to socializing and communicating with people who are comparable to them. They feel immediately uncomfortable like a fish out of water the moment that they are surrounded by people who are different from them. A significant part of your development and, in many cases, healing, occurs when you cross the track and relate to people who are ahead of you in some way. These relationships create a chance for you to grow.

Will they make fun of me? Some people who are more educated, more intellectual, more wealthy, or even more spiritual than we may deprecate us when we are in their company. Those people exist on all levels, but they are not the only ones there. If you have a bad experience, then move to the other side of the room. But do not allow anyone to drive you back into your old world.

"Suppose I don't measure up?" you ask. I know how you feel. But if you don't stand near a ruler, you won't know how far you need to grow or monitor how much you have developed. This is a natural reserve, but realize that if you have less information it doesn't mean that you are a lesser person. Life is a school, and every new acquaintance is a teacher. Whatever these individuals now know, they haven't always known it. The greatest indictment against not knowing is not learning. Seize this as a chance to learn.

Please do not try to pretend to know what you do not know. It is a terrible mistake to try to measure up by discussing what you do not know. I have seen countless people try to impress others who they were better off learning from in silence. My mother used to tell us, "If you keep your mouth shut, no one will know what you do not know." The truth is simple: Whenever you speak, you tell me more than you can imagine about who and what you are. It is better to speak genuinely and sincerely, asking questions when appropriate. Most people who are experts enjoy a chance to discuss and share what they know. The people worth knowing are those who do not seek an opportunity to belittle you. This is far better than trying to be a part of an elite discussion and thereby revealing that not only are you ignorant of the subject you are trying to discuss but that you are also too arrogant and small to yield to those who are more authoritative. Lack of knowledge is not criminal, but lack of wisdom can be lethal.

Being exposed to people who are further developed than you are is a gift. Use these opportunities wisely. When Providence causes your steps to go upward and climb the next rung of the ladder, these guidelines may prove to be very helpful so that you do not slip:

1. Do not shrink away people who have expertise or experiences that are new to you. Your insecurity can easily be misread as arrogance or some other unintended message.

2. Do not try to impress them by a camaflouged attempt to be an intellectual equal. If you are forced into discussions that intimidate you, listen when they are discussing what you do not know and ask questions when appropriate. When required to initiate conversation, always talk about what you know and listen attentively to what you do not know. The next time you meet, you will be that much ahead.

3. Do not keep coming to class without your homework. By that, I mean that when you see that God is taking you higher, start preparing yourself, your wardrobe, and your speech for the next level. The challenge will be exciting and exhilarating. A crash course may include a trusted friend who has some understanding of where you are going and where you are. This will be invaluable. These are people whom you may question and feel comfortable with. If there

are no such persons, read up until you get the basics. Use what you do know to help you understand what you do not know. Almost everything you will ever learn is related to something that you already know. That is why Jesus taught in parables. He used what we could understand to teach us what we did not.

4. Do not become prematurely presumptuous. Just because someone else knows her well enough to call her Helen, doesn't mean that you should. If you are going to err, err on the side of the formal, not the familiar. When using a name or title, refer to the person the way they introduce themselves to you. If a new acquaintance says, "Hello, my name is Charles," then don't say, "What's up, Charlie!" If they refer to their clergy as "Reverend," but you are accustomed to saying "Brother John," always remember that presumption can be irritating even when tolerated. Do not try to change the protocol of the environment to what you are used to. You are not where you were, and this may require that you acquire some versatility and dexterity in how you address or handle people. When in doubt, ask. It is better to ask than to be presumptuous. *How do you prefer that I address you? When calling back, is it more convenient for me to call you directly, or would you prefer that I address my concerns to someone on your staff?* These questions are always appropriate and appreciated.

Since the ways we act reveal so much about our life goals and how far along we are in our journey, there are certain things that one should do to ensure relational and societal standing. Now let me offer four do's to go with the don'ts:

1. Do give thanks to those who serve you. Do you usually send a thank you when you have been received, invited, or enhanced in some way? An expression of gratitude leaves a pleasant taste in the mouth of the person whom you have recently met. If someone has helped you with information, always acknowledge them.

2. Do avoid any actions that might be construed as opportunistic. Carry your own weight. Look for ways that you can make your presence a benefit and not a liability.

3. Do have a clear goal in your mind if you are going to do business or meet with a busy person. When you are in his or her company, be open and direct about what you need or desire. Rambling and sneaky approaches always assume that the person you are talking to is somehow less intelligent than you. That may be a lethal mistake. Never go to a business meeting with an important person without a clear understanding in your own mind of what you want to walk away from the table with. You cannot monitor success if you do not know your own goal.

4. Do get a clear, up-front understanding of the terms of your relationship. Always know what you want out of the relationship and what they want. Know when you want it and how you can both contribute to a successful, win-win approach to this mutual issue. This understanding of the parameters of the relationship will save you and them needless disappointments. Define what type of relationship it is and keep the conversation within the scope of what is appropriate for that kind of relationship. No one can catch a high ball in the living room. Keep the focus within the ballpark of what you are willing to do.

THE FUTURE IS NOW

Get ready now, my friend, for you are going into new arenas in the twenty-first century, and you may have to leave your past behind in order to embark on this new experience. New adventures of the spirit will take you into new settings and will require that you leave your comfort zone. God's blessing often takes us away from our comfort zones. It is often His will to bring new people into your life, and you can best ascertain where you are by who is around this new post to which you have been assigned. It is like the old railroad crossing sign. When you come to a railroad track, you will see signs that warn pedestrians and automobile drivers alike that occasionally trains will come down those tracks. It is not a sign to forbid you from crossing and going ahead as much as it is a sign designed to warn you to proceed with caution and alertness. As children we were taught to get quiet and watchful at these crossings. Although a warning siren would ring out distinctly whenever a train was approaching, my dad would roll down his window to be certain that no warning bell had escaped his hearing. The message was always the same: stop, look, and listen. Proceed with care.

As you cross from one social junction to the next, always remain attentive. But please don't spend the rest of your life stuck on one side of the tracks for fear of calamity if you cross to the other side. It is important that you proceed with care, but for God's sake, do proceed. Too many people stay on the safe side of the tracks, but they miss the once-in-a-life opportunity to experience and learn new aspects about themselves, others, and the world around us. They miss it because they are intimidated by people and afraid of making mistakes. You *will* make mistakes; we all do. The points that I shared with you will help you to minimize them, but there will be no alleviating all of them. To err is human. So allow yourself the right to be wrong, and to laugh at your mistakes but profit from them.

The most important thing is that you do not allow your life to be lived in an invisible bubble. Many people are quarantined from real life, incubated in a vacuum filled with people who are just like them. Many of us are just dying of sheer, unadulterated boredom. Expand your horizons, discover the world. You don't have to travel across the globe to discover another world; there is probably one right across the street or across town. There is another world at the country club or volunteer center. There is another world at the ballet or the baseball field.

So what if your expedition takes you beyond your normal level of life? So what if you find yourself at an intersection of life facing the possibility of crossing into an unknown territory? Calmly remember to stop, look, and listen. These three simple rules that protect us as we cross the street or the railroad tracks are applicable for us as we cross over into new arenas of life.

USHERS OF LIFE

As we travel beyond our limitations, we will meet new people. These people are ushers who are placed at various stations in your life to enlarge you and assist you in developing beyond your meager horizons. They assist you in maximizing your life, loves, and interests. Do not ignore them. They are God's messengers. They are often used to open doors, expedite processes, insure safe passage, and neutralize your fears as you travel this brief tour of the planet we call Earth.

Let me introduce you to an usher on assignment, sent to a young girl who needed aid in adjusting to a new world:

So Ruth the Moabitess said to Naomi, "Please let me go to the field, and glean heads of grain after him in whose sight I may find favor." And she said to her, "Go, my daughter." Then she left, and went and gleaned in the field after the reapers. And she happened to come to the part of the field belonging to Boaz, who was of the family of Elimelech. Now behold, Boaz came from Bethlehem, and said to the reapers, "The LORD be with you!" And they answered him, "The LORD bless you!" (Ruth 2:2–4, NKJV)

Ruth the Moabitess was new to Bethlehem. She wasn't used to the way they did things, but she pushed herself out to learn by association. She began by gleaning behind those who were reaping. You would be surprised how much you can pick up about anything just by listening. Like Ruth, you can glean behind those who are more advanced and work your way up. If you want to elevate yourself, associate with those who have matriculated into the areas that you aspire to, and catch what they drop until you have caught up with what they have. You will find that there are little nuggets that can be picked up quite easily if you care to stick around.

Ruth stayed close to an older woman named Naomi. Naomi knew the ropes. It is important to associate with people who know the ropes. If you "stay in your league," you will lose every game. Naomi was different. She was a different nationality, she was a different age, and at a different stage of maturity. I imagine there were times when Ruth said silly things in comparison to this older woman's ideas and wisdoms. There were no doubt times when they didn't relate to each other. But differences and distinctions were put here by God to destroy boredom and bring forth growth.

Naomi was perfect to usher Ruth into a deeper stage of life. What made Naomi particularly attractive was the fact that she understood both where Ruth had been and also where she was currently. I believe that one of the most difficult relationships to find is the relationship in which the other person can appreciate and respect both where you have been and where you are now.

Those persons who understand your past are essential because, try all we want to avoid it, we are largely a product of our past. It shapes many of our likes and dislikes, eccentricities and peculiarities. In short, it has all the world to do with how you react now. But having someone who "knew you when" is not enough, as many lack the dexterity to relate to where you are now. Most people "knew you when," but they often have a tendency to anchor you to their previous knowledge of you and thereby stifle your growth. If they themselves haven't progressed, your development is often seen as betrayal, and they resent you. Only a very secure minority has the capacity to grow with you. If they haven't kept up with you, they will inevitably try to drag you back to their last impression of you.

Then there are those people who know where you are now but do not know where you came from, and therefore can't always be objective in their current appreciation of your struggle and process, values and fears. No one can appreciate the enormity of your success if they haven't seen the ferocity of your struggle. It is like walking into a theater in the middle of the play where you keep asking, "What does he mean by that?" Or, "Why is she so upset about that?" You have missed a major portion of the setup, and hence you do not fully appreciate the present.

Naomi could both appreciate the past and recognize the present. If Ruth had tried to assimilate to her new environment without the benefit of someone who knew both her past and present, it would have been much harder. Naomi was a sighted woman leading a blind woman through the maze of a new experience. Naomi was Ruth's eyes into a world that she didn't know. She was her tutor, her mentor, and her guide in avoiding foolish mistakes.

Ruth had left her homeland of Moab, come to Bethlehem, and was confronted with all sorts of new rules, laws, religions, and social ideologies. God had brought her into a place for which she felt ill-prepared. He had brought her into a place where she was going to have to lean and depend on God as well as on who God had sent into her life. She was like Dorothy in the land of Oz—she needed direction.

Have you ever had God bless you and you found yourself in a strange new world that was unfamiliar? I tell you, being blessed can be stressful. Who are these people? What should I say to them? Should I take this position or hold out for another? Who can I trust over here in Oz? The blessing of the Lord will make you lie down at night and think to yourself, "This is a long way from Kansas." It *is* a long way from Kansas, but you can handle it. Always remember: If you are going to the promised land, you must leave home.

LIONS AND TIGERS AND BEARS, OH MY

When Dorothy landed in Oz, she was met by new friends, but she encountered new enemies as well. She walked through the woods afraid of the lions and tigers and bears. Like Dorothy, when God moves us out of the familiar, we will also face new predators. But not to worry; God will take care of us.

> Forget the former things; do not dwell on the past. See, I am doing a new thing! Now it springs up; do you not perceive it? I am making a way in the desert and streams in the wasteland. The wild animals honor me, the jackals and the owls, because I provide water in the desert and streams in the wasteland, to give drink to my people, my chosen, the people I formed for myself that they may proclaim my praise. (Isaiah 43:18–21, NIV)

God said in the twentieth verse that He can control the lions and tigers and bears. He does that so you don't have to sit at home chewing your nails and missing the opportunities that He has for you because of your fear of the predators in the unfamiliar terrain. These predators may be frightening, but God is using them to herald you into your destiny. He even uses the wicked witches that come after you when you change. They do not know it, but their hatred of you helps to drive you closer into your destiny. God often uses negative influences to assist Him in executing His plans. Your mission, should you decide to accept it, is to trust Him in new places like you did in the familiar ones. He will lead you safely and successfully out of Kansas and into your promised land.

FOLLOW THE
YELLOW BRICK ROAD

I have found that, basically, people are people anywhere you go. The rules might be different, the culture more diverse, but the basic pattern of people is similar. Like Dorothy, you will soon find that the new people remind you of persons from back home. They are the same, yet different. They are different, yet they are the same. Some more eccentric, others more intellectual, but these are just the trappings of life. Beneath that, people in Oz are a lot like those in Kansas. I have learned, as I have traveled the world ministering, teaching, and motivating, that beyond ethnic distinctions like skin tones, hair textures, and style preferences, we are all basically people. We are people whose personalities are a direct derivative of our own experiences, prejudices, and fears. And we all have little prejudices. They are not always racial. Some are intellectual. Some are theological. Some are cultural, but all are limiting. They limit us from enjoying the entire smorgasbord of life's variances. So as you go forward, do not feel so much like a stranger. You know more about these people than you think you do.

In light of all I have just told you, you may be asking, "Why go out there to meet them if people are all the same?" I am glad you asked that question. They are the same on the inside, but their experiences are not. It is their experiences that enlarge you and help you. Learn from others' experiences so that you can have your own.

I can't help but feel like I am preparing leaders for the twenty-first century. I feel as though I am called to prepare you for new horizons. You are going to move beyond Kansas. You are going to emerge into new worlds with new challenges. Ruth's Kansas was Moab. That was her homeland. Everything there was familiar. It was her comfort zone. But her promised land required that she travel outside of the familiar. Your Kansas might be an old job, an old neighborhood, or a past relationship. Leave Kansas and find the glory that God has promised you.

I have had the good pleasure of traveling halfway around the world, sitting at the table with aristocracy, being entertained by foreign dignitaries, and entertaining the fabulous and famous, and after having done it all I thought: "Boy, you have come a long way from your meager beginnings." In other words, I thought, "This sure ain't Kansas!" But as I reflect on the people I met and the real depth of who they were, I know that through these stretches and new experiences I have a deeper, richer life.

So you decide. Do you want to stay at home with the mediocre and milk the proverbial cows, or do you want to click your heels on the yellow brick road? As for me, I wear a size thirteen!

THIRTEEN

GOOD TO
THE LAST DROP

My mother was possibly one of the best cooks I have ever known. She was also the prettiest woman on the planet, or so I thought at nine years old. Her light-blue, subtly printed dresses, ordered from J. C. Penney's catalog, were simple and not particularly glamorous. But they were always pressed and starched crisp and clean. Her smile was the starburst in the ugly little kitchen in which she cooked. I have glorious memories of my mother in that kitchen, but one of my most vivid mental snapshots is of her standing in front of the old formica table, and laid on it in front of her were bags of flour, vanilla extract, a dozen eggs, a sifter, a bag of sugar, two sticks of butter, two cups of sugar, and a large bowl. I can still see the underside of her arm jiggle as she took the flat end of a spoon and creamed the sugar into the butter. She was preparing a pound cake that would ultimately smell up the whole house.

I loved to watch her bake. I sat in the kitchen smelling the wonderful smells and listening to her chattering about the hot subjects of the times. I watched her as she beat the eggs, whipped the batter, and poured it all into a Bundt pan whose paint was worn off and whose sides were burned black. She would slide the pan into the oven, and in less than an hour she would pull out the family's favorite treat. But I wasn't in that hot kitchen waiting for the cake to bake. Oh sure, I already knew that I would whine after dinner for a second piece. But the real reason I sat waiting in that poorly ventilated inferno of a kitchen was hope. I hoped that when she had scraped all the batter that she could from the bowl, I might be given the bowl to lick. It was the same scenario every time. She would turn to place her tattered bunt pan into the oven and I would sit up like a puppy. She would laugh and, not even bothering to turn around, she would say over her shoulder, "Go ahead." With one swoop, which would have made Michael Jordan envious, I would leap forward and lunge after the almost empty bowl. I would run my fingers around the edge like a starving orphan given some scraps. I would get that bowl so clean I saw no real need to wash it, though I am sure my mother might disagree. With my fingers in the bowl and batter smudged across my cheeks, I learned what it took me years to articulate: We can find such joy if we endeavor to get the most out of everything.

SAVOR IT ALL

I guess to some degree I am still scraping the bowl of life and enjoying the residuals that others might have thought were insignificant. You see, all of life is good. If you want to enjoy your life to the fullest, don't just wait on something that's baking in the oven. Get the bowl while you wait and get something out of every part of the process. People who learn to scrape the bowl wait without hunger because things that others ignore have nourished them. Most people miss the best part of every adventure. They wait for the main event and miss the scraps. It is in the residue that we often find the best part.

I am reminded of First and Second Timothy. I believe that Paul's final correspondence to his spiritual son Timothy contained a message to teach his son to always absorb and retain the parts that others wouldn't appreciate. Let's consider the scene and try to imagine what might have happened when Paul's gospel apprentice received a correspondence that would teach him the value of scraping the bowl. Let's go into the young boy's house and see what lessons we can learn.

LETTER IN THE NIGHT

It was late in the evening. Timothy was about to turn in for the evening, when suddenly, the silence is broken by a series of knocks rapping wildly on the door. Who would call on him at this hour of the night? The knock grew more insistent, so Timothy hustled to the door before they knocked it down. "Just a minute, please!" He opened the creaking door and peered out into the evening air. There stood a young carrier boy holding out a parcel. The boy's face was flushed, and he seemed out of breath. Panting as he spoke, he said, "You have a letter, sir."

Timothy was surprised to get mail this late in the evening. Who would send me something so urgent that it could not wait until morning delivery? he may have wondered to himself. When Timothy saw the handwriting, he quickly snatched the parcel from the young lad and sent him away. Hurriedly he closed the door, eager to read what news the letter brought. Timothy sat on the bed, and with trembling hands he opened the parcel. It was a letter, written on dark, soiled paper. The handwriting was weak, the paper wrinkled and frayed, but it was unmistakably a letter from Paul!

Paul had become a mentor who had greatly assisted the young Timothy as he developed his new Christian character. Some call it discipling, and I guess that was what Timothy aspired to be—a disciple of

Jesus, mentored by Paul. What a responsibility to be known as the spiritual son of a man who was as awesome, educated, infinitely articulate, and powerful as the apostle Paul. He was intellectual and culturally diversified. He was respected and revered by some of the greatest theologians and scholars of his day. Timothy greatly respected him, but he feared that his opportunities to sit at his feet were coming to a close. Lately he had not seen much of his mentor, as Paul was being persecuted for his bold speeches. Sometimes Timothy wondered if Paul was going to make it. Even this letter had been written from a jail cell, where Paul was facing yet another set of charges of insurrection and heresy.

Timothy glanced down at the letter and there, written in larger script, were the compelling words, "Come before winter." These words would haunt him all of his life. They seemed to smell of death itself. It would appear that the old man knew that his time was coming to a close. Timothy hastily read the rest of the letter, pausing a few moments here and there to reflect on the weighted words the sage had written. He could almost hear Paul's voice speaking through the tattered pages of this correspondence.

When he had finished reading the letter, Timothy was puzzled. Here was Paul in terrible trouble with the law, and yet he seemed unmoved by it. He seemed aware but disinterested in what seemed like the sure death sentence that awaited him. Maybe he knew something, Timothy thought. Maybe he had had a word from the Lord. He had undoubtedly survived many such threatening times. Timothy reflected on a letter the old man had written to Corinth, in which he had listed a few of his hair-raising experiences. Paul's life had been full of adventure.

Are they ministers of Christ? (I speak as a fool) I am more; in labours more abundant, in stripes above measure, in prisons more frequent, in deaths oft. Of the

Jews five times received I forty stripes save one. Thrice was I beaten with rods, once was I stoned, thrice I suffered shipwreck, a night and a day I have been in the deep; In journeyings often, in perils of waters, in perils of robbers, in perils by mine own countrymen, in perils by the heathen, in perils in the city, in perils in the wilderness, in perils in the sea, in perils among false brethren; In weariness and painfulness, in watching often, in hunger and thirst, in fastings often, in cold and nakedness. Beside those things that are without, that which cometh upon me daily, the care of all the churches. Who is weak, and I am not weak? Who is offended, and I burn not? If I must needs glory, I will glory of the things which concern mine infirmities. (2 Corinthians 11:23–30, KJV)

Maybe this recent bout with the authorities would end up being just another incident in a long string of near-disasters that Paul had survived. But Timothy was also puzzled by Paul's requests. He didn't ask for a good lawyer, which would seem to be the logical choice. Instead, the old man only asked for more paper, a book, and a coat. Paul had only asked him for what he needed. He had realized most of his purpose, and he was comfortable with this winter season in his life. His life had all the earmarks of real success. He knew who he was in life. He knew where he was in life. He knew why he was there. To know these things is the essence of self-assurance and fulfillment. Without these answers, one dies incomplete.

Yes, Paul knew exactly what he needed and when he needed it. The old mentor's words echoed in Timothy's brain: "Come before winter." Timothy had to go soon no matter what the expense or even the danger. He had to take only the three things his beloved father-figure had asked of him.

Bring the cloak that I left with Carpus at Toas when you come—and the books, especially the parchments. (2 Timothy 4:13, NKJV)

COAT OF COMFORT

You, like Timothy, might also think Paul's requests are strange. But let me explain it to you. He doesn't ask for attorneys, because real purpose needs no defense. It is what it is. History tires more accurately and with more justice than any counsel of our peers in any generation. Time will tell the world who you are and what you did, honestly and objectively. Paul had grown beyond trying to justify himself before men who would never grasp the scope of his calling or the magnitude of his convictions. There is a calmness that should come with experience. Paul is secure in his convictions and doesn't need legal representation to speak for him. No, all Paul asks for are the three things that we all ultimately need to finish our race and complete our purpose: a coat, a book, and more paper.

The coat is a covering. When you are in your later years, you desire a coat, for you want a place you can go to for warmth against the chill of winter. Think of workaholic businessmen who spend their prime always at the office, on the phone or making another deal. In their later years, many of them turn to their wives, who they all but ignored in their frantic race to success. As they near the mark of completion, they realize that the prize does not mean that much if they have no one to share it with in their final days. They, in a newly acquired sense of wisdom, seek the coat of love and affection to insulate them from the piercing, howling winds of the winter of life.

We all need a coat throughout our lives to protect us from the unavoidable adversity that life inevitably brings. We need the loving, covering insulation to comfort our hearts when we are challenged by the demands placed on us as we make our way through the world. A coat doesn't distract you from your purpose but gives you comfort while you complete your course. If you can have a coat of comfort, some place or hobby, some relaxing thing that gives you joy, you can avoid harmful distractions and keep yourself faithful to your life's path. There are countless men and women who just needed a coat. They needed a hug, but ended up in an affair. They needed a vacation, but they ended up quitting their jobs. Sometimes, when we fail to get what we need, we end up doing something foolish and dangerous for the lack of a coat. We especially need a coat in the winter of our lives, as the chill is the greatest, the landscape bleak. A warm coat of love and safety will carry us through the season and enable us to reach our final destination triumphantly.

Tragically, some people don't have anyone who can bring them a coat. There are those who have been hurt before and fear being forsaken again, so they are leary of people and don't allow anyone to be near them. For others, their incessant need for control stops them from appearing vulnerable enough to admit their need to anyone. They may feel too proud to say, "Yes, I have arrived 'there' and I am a success, but I still need the warmth and covering of a coat." Even Jesus cried out from the cross. There are times you know you are right where you are supposed to be, but you still want someone to bring you some meager offering of comfort and expression of love. Jesus asked for wine. Paul asked for a coat. All of us need someone who can reach us with some comfort as we face new challenges. Paul's challenge was the one of nearing the end of his life. Yours might be the challenge of facing a new venture. But each of us faces some thing that makes us need a coat.

BOOK OF LIFE

Paul also asked for a book. You might say, "Isn't that a strange thing for a man who is sitting on death row to ask for?" Sometimes, in spite of where we are, we have to continue to move forward as best we can with what we have at our disposal. Are you using all that you have at your disposal to maximize a situation you cannot change? If you must be in the situation, it is imperative that you make the best of it. Yes, Paul, the great man of faith and power, realized that although he had escaped many tragedies, he was now sitting on death row. Perhaps he had come to grips with the ages and stages of life. Perhaps he had recognized that though he had been invincible and resourceful, anointed and profoundly gifted, alas, he was still nonetheless mortal.

At the risk of sounding morbid, I ask: Are we not all on death row? Are we not all playing one huge game of beat the clock with life? It is generally about halfway through the game that the participants recognize that we are all eventually going to run out of time. This is what we often call mid-life crises. The crisis is the fact that the clock has more time to tick than the participants of the game have life left to play. The crisis is the fact that as we live life, we can see more promised land with our eye than we can walk with our foot. Isn't that why we can never truly have success without a successor? Isn't it true that what we really want to see our children do is benefit from our vision partially because we can see farther than we can reach? Are we not all like Moses, who stood on the top of Mount Nebo and saw a promised land that his feet were too frail and his body too mortal to reach? We need to write like Paul did and say, "Come before winter," come so I can pass on the nuggets of my wisdom and show you what I see.

But what makes Paul good to the last drop is not just his willingness to pass his mantle on to another man. What makes him great is not merely his ability to know who, what, where, and why, he was. What makes Paul good to the last drop is that when he recognized his mortality, he didn't stop living and cuddle up in a coat and set his eyes toward heaven. No, he was a man that maximizes moments. He said if this is it, then before I go I want to lick the bowl. He sends for a book because he is alive. And as long as you are alive, you must continue to feed your mind. Paul purposed in his heart that he was going to continue to feed his mind to the very last day. He asked for a book to show you and me that even on death row we must live life to the fullest.

Whether we live in a mansion or a dungeon, we still have an obligation to maximize each day. Each day, no, each second of every minute, is a gift from God. If we are going to maximize each moment, we must keep feeding our minds. Your mind needs fresh challenges. So Paul the great teacher sat on a cold floor in a jailhouse. He didn't ask for better accommodations, for he had learned whatever state he was in, therewith to be content. He knew that the stages and ages of life are what they are. He knew it was no use for old men to wish to be young, or short men to crave to be tall. He had learned that contentment is the greatest gift of maturity. He just wanted his books so that he could keep feeding himself. Reading was his request for a last meal. It is the smorgasbord of the soul. If you are going to maximize your life, do not stop learning!

Some would say, "Why learn more when you are not getting out of jail and you are going to die?" Knowledge should not be acquired like fine jewelry to be flaunted to impress others. We should keep learning througout our lives because knowledge keeps our minds sharp and our souls free. Paul knew that even though he was locked in a jail cell, reading afforded him the freedom to transcend his situation and explore new worlds.

I do not know what book Paul requested, but I do know that his motive for reading could not have been to develop some impressive rhetoric for his next speaking engagement. This pursuit had little to do with others; it was more about his habits remaining unbroken by his circumstances. Do not allow life to break you. No matter where you are and what you are enduring, even if you face an uncertain end, you are not there yet. Maximize each moment and enjoy it to the last drop.

LAST WILL AND TESTAMENT

Paul's last request of Timothy is that he bring some paper. This is perhaps my favorite item of the three. I am amazed and awed by the paper for several reasons. One of them is that in the face of impending danger, Paul ignores his crisis and seizes the chance to continue to be productive. He asked for paper because he is relentless enough to say to his captors just before they behead him, "I have something else that I want to say. I'm not done yet." I admire it because he spares no time for tears. There is no final tear-jerking, gut-wrenching display of self-pity. No, Paul keeps his sight steady and his heart strong, and continues to push forward to fulfill his purpose.

Unlike the book request, which challenges us to keep receiving, the request for paper challenges us to keep giving. The art of living is to keep giving until the end. Jesus on the cross, with nails piercing his hands and feet, continues to minister. Ignoring his own malady, he seizes the opportunity to serve others. Here is the secret antidote for life's hard places. It is not the taking in alone; it is the incessant, relentless giving that keeps life meaningful and rich.

I am reminded of a time recently when my mother's brothers came to visit me. Most of them are in their seventies and eighties. They are all tall and still stand erect and appear quite in control of their faculties. They gave me some seasoned advice that seemed the opposite of all that I had been taught. They said, "Whatever you do, do not retire!" I thought, "What in the world do you mean?" Today we are constantly being told to prepare for disability, retirement, and life after sixty-five. Yet here were all my uncles saying that the one thing they regretted was retiring. I was amazed. I had always pictured myself at seventy, still strong and vibrant, sitting on the edge of the incoming tide of some Hawaiian island, drinking pineapple juice out of a coconut and reflecting on the relativity of issues and the real essence of human development. I had it all planned, right down to the baby-blue Hawaiian shirt with white Bermuda shorts showing my wrinkled knees, allowing them to tan into a deeper shade of brown!

But my dear uncles screamed in unified assent. They said to stay in the game until the last second and never go sit on the bench. It seems that it is their opinion that once you sit down, you can't get up. They said that life loses meaning when you subconsciously tell yourself you are finished. Like Paul they told me to keep working until the end.

I thought about their words. And I think of Paul and wonder if it wasn't so much that he was afraid of not getting up, but that he was simply not ready to sit down—he was still in the game. Maybe he had such a relationship with God that he was still receiving revelation even in the final hours of his life. I think he was still spooning out the treasure that was deeply brewed in the caldron of his human soul. It was obviously more important than any danger that he faced. It was too good to be left in the proverbial pot of his thought-life. Could it be that his sage wisdom reached its finest hours after having simmered for years in his life's experiences and that he wanted to record the last few teaspoons of wisdom before he went on to his reward?

He cries out for Timothy to slip him a few parcels of paper beneath the door into the dark, dank atmosphere of his prison because God wasn't through with him yet. He wanted to be sure that up until the last moments of his life he was serving God's will. As profound as his statements were, my purpose for mentioning them is not to rehash what he said but to remind you that he did his best writing on the eve of his execution. In the face of that kind of terror, he still chooses to recognize his worth over his plight. He maximizes his life in the face of death. I want you to recognize that the greatest threads of wisdom are not just hidden in what he said but also in when he said it.

The old father of truth was teaching his son the most important lesson that a person can learn by showing him, not just telling him. His message was to never get out of the game. Even in the last remaining seconds of the game, a touchdown is still possible. He was teaching his son to ignore danger and scoff at defeat. He knew that what a young person needs to hear the most from their father is simply, do not quit!

> *They will turn their ears away from the truth and turn aside to myths. But you, keep your head in all situations, endure hardship, do the work of an evangelist, discharge all the duties of your ministry. For I am already being poured out like a drink offering, and the time has come for my departure. I have fought the good fight, I have finished the race, I have kept the faith. Now there is in store for me the crown of righteousness, which the Lord, the righteous Judge, will award to me on that day— and not only to me, but also to all who have longed for his appearing. Do your best to come to me quickly . . . (2 Timothy 4:4–10, NIV)*

In the final hours, as the curtains began to close on his life, Paul scribbles madly the last few sentences of wisdom that would rock the world. He reflects upon his existence and uses a metaphor whereby he compares his life to the priestly act of a drink offering. The drink offering was the pouring out of wine from a glass. When Paul says that the time is come for him to be poured out like a drink offering, he means that he has given himself to his cause. He considers every act he performed a moment in which he gave just a little more of himself. His life was like the slow emptying out of a glass of wine. He gave his wisdom, his thoughts, his words—he gave all that he was.

Might I suggest to you that every encounter and accomplishment in life costs us something. No one attains anything without some type of expenditure. The reality is that all successes, and even failures, cause us to spend moments that will never be regained. When older people look at their loved ones and say, "I am tired," it is not the weariness of someone who needs sleep. It is the depleting of a spent life. They are experiencing the emptying out of the glass that started full of promise and potential. They are reflecting on the fact that drip by drip, day by day, they have been lifted like a glass. Finally, Paul says he is like a glass offered up, the ultimate and final toast. It reminds me of a child who, in an endeavor to get the last drops of milk out of a glass, turns it completely upside down. It is the same emptying out that Paul is experiencing. God has decided to take him home, and Paul offers himself up.

Age is not the issue. Purpose determines when one is to be offered up. Jesus was offered up at the ripe young age of thirty-three. It is not a chronological date that determines when you are offered. It is the sensitivity to God's purpose that causes you to sense that this is it, I am down to the last drop. Paul wants to make sure that he is as effective in the last hours as he was in the first. There is nothing worse than getting to the bottom of a coffee cup and tasting the bitter grinds that are stuck at the bottom. It ruins the whole experience of drinking from the cup in the first place. Paul longs to avoid these dregs at the bottom of the cup. Many men have ruined their lives in their latter years. Be careful how you finish the race. For the last drops will be remembered long after the life span is ended.

The other issue that is extremely significant here is the incredible expense of living. Paul suggests to Timothy that everything he did took a little bit more out of him. Each day we live, each experience we encounter, requires another drop. That is why we must be so careful what we do and who we spend our lives with. The fact of the matter is, we are literally spending our lives. You must evaluate the worth and necessity of each person. What will be the level of your involvement with them? How much of you are you willing to spend to maintain this relationship? You see, my friend, you are literally spending yourself. After this, there will be no more of you. Paul had been wise enough not to spend himself on things that did not matter. He knew how to maximize his moments and he, from the jail cell, reports to Timothy, I have kept the faith. I have finished my course, and now, as I am about to be offered up, I share my last few drops with you.

THE FINAL TALLY

Who will you spend your last drops with? And what cause have you dedicated your expenditures to? What noble commitment have you aligned yourself to, or are you just existing each day in a lethargic state of apathy and indifference? If you are, you are wasting your drops. You are losing the life's blood of your existence. What a sad malady to end your life and not know where you spent your last drops.

It is traditionally believed that Paul's condemnation and execution occurred during the persecution of Christians under the Roman emperor Nero. But being martyred could in no way destroy his works. If anything, it enhanced them all the more. It is widely accepted that the site of his execution may be viewed at Tre Fontane, on the Ostian Road. His tomb is in the Basilica of St. Paul Outside the Walls. There, beneath the high altar, is a stone inscription going back to at least the fourth century: "To Paul, Apostle and Martyr."

Imagine, then, Paul spending his final flickering moments on earth scribbling wildly the last few thoughts that would shape the face of Christianity as we know it today. Imagine him in final hours, on feeble knees, strapped like an animal, living in a caged environment but still dripping truth in the face of evil. As he lies trembling on the cold, hard stone ground of his cell, he writes a testimony to his protégé, suggesting to him that the struggle was worth it. It is in our final moments of life that we give the purest milk from the breasts of our experience. If we are going to ever reveal our truest heart, it is in the face of death, for it is there that we have absolutely no possible intimidation. What can they do to threaten a dying man? The police take very seriously death-bed confessions, for they realize that the words of the dying are filled with sober truth. It is from this lofty height of spiritual integrity that Paul pens his final thoughts, defines his own eulogy, and dies with his finger pointing a dying world back to the cross.

Perhaps it was his struggles that perked him like a pot of coffee into the rich elixir that had been such a source of strength for his community and such a legacy for his son. The pain had been the fire that had brewed him, and now he was ready to be served. His contribution is still impacting the world. He touched a world that he didn't even know. He challenged people whom he would never meet. He inspired greatness from the ashes of mediocrity. That, to me, is the measure of effective living. What will most resonate about you when your voice is hushed by death itself? What will you be remembered for the most? So many men and women have licked the cup of Paul's life that he would be awed that so much taste could come from the wise use of so little time.

From the stone-covered floors of his jail cell Paul's resounding voice effects change. He is a man whose blood would spatter wildly across the pages of the epistles. His life, though lost, was found. His meaning could not be silenced. He had succeeded in his final hour in teaching one final lecture. He taught in his final moments the most profound truth. You see, it is not how well we start that matters most. Ultimately, it is how effectively we finish that leaves an indelible imprint in the sand of time. We must, with all of our might, attempt to protect ourselves in latter years as much as we did in early ones. You see, people will forget all the good you did over one thing done wrong at the end. I know it is not right and perhaps it seems unfair. But it is, nevertheless, still true. The old man lives long enough and stands bright enough to teach the young man, who has already started his life. He doesn't just teach him how to begin. For starting is not enough. He teaches him how to end.

The end of a thing is better than its beginning; the patient in spirit is better than the proud in spirit. (Ecclesiastes 7:8, NKJV)

What a grand finale. Paul ends his life in a crescendo of wisdom and triumph. In his final hours he seeks little, gives much, and dies without desecrating all that he has lived for. When the book was closed, the coat folded, and the final notation inscribed, the old man had maintained his integrity and retained his proficiency. With an upward gaze and a firm conviction, he faced Nero's chopping block. It was there that he was beheaded and thereby relieved of his duties.

He leaves a scholarship of thought handed to the heart of his successor. And this is what he leaves to you, this is his simple message: It doesn't matter how you start. It only matters how you finish. Success is achieved when the final tally comes in, and it is said, "What ever happened to him?" And the reply is made, "Oh, I thought you knew. He's gone now. But I have to tell you one thing. That old boy was better than Maxwell House."

May it be said of us as it can be of Paul: "He was good to the last drop!"

THE TIME OF YOUR LIFE

I began this book by looking at a life cut down in its prime, the great life of President John F. Kennedy. Now, before I even finish this book, his only son, John Fitzgerald Kennedy, Jr., has died in a tragic plane crash at sea, along with his lovely wife and her sister. No one but the Lord knew the appointment those three young people would have that hazy summer night off the coast of Massachusetts. John-John, the little boy who we all knew and loved, the solemn saluter of his own father's farewell, was suddenly no more a live part of this world. His hyphen had come to an end: There was now a year to put on the right hand side of his life: 1960–1999.

No one would have guessed it. No one could have imagined that a young, healthy, wealthy, generous, kind, intelligent man like JFK, Jr., could suddenly be here one moment and then be taken the next. Like his father, he leaves behind a hyphen that seems too short to us. So much energy, passion, and intensity—so much success—reduced once again to a small part of a line.

The Preacher in Ecclesiastes tells us that death comes for the wise and foolish alike, for the rich and the poor, the righteous and the wicked. We will all perish. The only time we have, my friend, is right *now*. Now is the time to take responsibility for each and every moment. Now is the time to stop settling for less than you are called to be. Now is the time when you either jump on board the train or you stay at the station. Now is the time of your life.

When I was a boy, I could not wait to be a grown man. Time seemed to drag on and on—how much longer until I could date, until I could drive, until I could work, until I could marry, lead a church, raise children, and on and on. Then, as a young man, I couldn't wait to charge into becoming who God had called me to be. I wanted to embrace His definition of success for me, to pursue the best use of my gifts and abilities for His kingdom, and He has blessed me for it. Now, as I reach the middle of my life, suddenly time has started to shift. Like the children's game of Musical Chairs, the music has started going faster and faster, and the number of chairs remaining gets fewer and fewer. There seems to never be enough time to accomplish the tasks of each day. As my head hits the pillow well into the night for a few hours rest, I ask myself what I've really accomplished that day. Sometimes it is clearly a successful day: Much work was given and much fruit was produced. Many other times, however, the day seems to have consisted of two steps forward and three steps back. I worked hard, but nothing seemed to be completed, nothing seemed to be accomplished as well as it could or should. On these days, the only way I know that I have succeeded is because I compare it to the vision God has given me for what I am to do.

Like the builder who must check the construction of each wall with the master blueprint for the house, we, too, must continually consult our blueprints for success. If we are not diligent to know where we are going and how we are to get there, then we will end up with a lot of walls, but no floors, roofs, doors, or windows. We must measure each day by how we have furthered the journey toward our destiny. Even on days that frustrate us, or that seem to have been wasted, we must press on and trust that God will use those days to bring other days to harvest.

We do not have much time left, my friend. I am not trying to scare you or pressure you. I am simply trying to help you see clearly. The time of your life is right now, the very moment your eyes are scanning this page. Shortly, in just a matter of a minute or two, you will finish the last page of this book and get up and go about the business of your life, whatever that may be. You may turn out the light and roll over in bed for a night's sleep. You may get off the plane and prepare for that big meeting. You may rise from your chair and begin to prepare the evening meal. Whatever you will do after the cover is closed, wherever you go, whoever you are, please hear the sound of my benediction to you.

Maximize each and every moment of your life from here on out. Do not let anyone or anything deter you from your purpose. As I have tried to help you see throughout these pages, evaluate your relationships, your career, your choices, but hold fast the vision of yourself crossing the finish line, knowing that you have run the race with the bold integrity of who you are. Only you can run the race to be yourself successfully. It is a different kind of competition. No other runners are breathing down your neck; there is only the shadow of yourself if you do not pursue the prize. The race is against yourself to be who our Creator has made you to be. Embrace this journey with the total passion of your mind, heart, and soul.

Persevere, my friend, and may the Lord God bless you in all your endeavors as you stretch and strain, sprint and crawl, laugh and cry toward the final destiny that He sets before you. Maximize these moments and make this the best time of your life!